HIGH FINANCE
God's Financial Plan
Tithes and Offerings

HIGH FINANCE
God's Financial Plan
Tithes and Offerings

by
Frederick K. C. Price

HARRISON HOUSE
Tulsa, Oklahoma

Unless otherwise indicated,
all Scripture quotations are taken from
the *King James Version* of the Bible.

4th Printing
Over 30,000 in Print

HIGH FINANCE—God's Financial Plan—
Tithes and Offerings
ISBN 0-89274-326-3
Copyright © 1984 by Frederick K. C. Price
Crenshaw Christian Center
P. O. Box 90000
Los Angeles, California 90009

Published by Harrison House, Inc.
P. O. Box 35035
Tulsa, Oklahoma 74153

Printed in the United States of America.

Contents

1
God Has A Plan
He Wants You To Prosper

Different companies advertise certain kinds of financial programs and plans, all designed to help us utilize our monies wisely for our future. These financial plans are designed so that when we reach retirement age, the end of our working years, we will have a nest egg to live on.

Many people do not realize that Almighty God has a financial plan for His people. The financial plan Almighty God has for His children begins in the now and carries through eternity.

People become very skiddish when you talk about tithes and offerings. The first thing they say is: "Oh, Lord, there he goes! That preacher wants my money. What scheme does he have to take my money from me?"

I am really not interested in getting your money. I am interested in you! I want to be an assist or a channel, by the Holy Spirit, to get your life into a proper relationship with the Father God through Jesus Christ. Once you come into a knowledge of how to walk in the Word of faith and power, I do not have to be concerned about getting your money. You will freely be a giver into the Kingdom of God.

I am interested in you, not in your money. Besides that, I cannot get it from you unless I steal it or you give it to me. I am not going to steal it, because I would be in violation of the Word of God, which says, "Thou shalt not steal."

If you are scared that a preacher is going to get your money, all you have to do is keep your money in your pocket. It is just that simple. Keep it in your pocket, then I cannot get it.

God has a financial plan and the Body of Christ needs to find out about it. One reason God has been unable to do more in this area is because the people of God have lived in a poverty syndrome. You see, it costs money to proclaim the Word of God. The Gospel (salvation) is free, but it costs big money for the pipeline to get the message to the people.

Example: Television. Television, whether you know it or not, is God's invention. There are many things that God has brought into being which the Church has not had enough sense to take advantage of, so the devil has ended up controlling the whole thing.

Television was not invented for the world; it was invented for the proclamation of the Gospel. Did you know that? Well, if you did not, you know it now! You probably thought television was invented by the devil, but it was not! The devil has never invented anything but confusion.

Television is a product of the mind of God with one purpose: to proclaim the Gospel. But because the Church of Jesus Christ, through religion, tradition, and denominationalism, has had such a narrow view of things, we have allowed the devil to come in, steal television and use it for devilish purposes instead of for the proclamation of the Gospel.

You can reach more people in one hour on television than you can by any other method. Today, through satellite communications, a program can be broadcast throughout the world at the same time. It would take fifty years for a person to physically go to every city. Through television we can be there in one hour. But it costs big money!

I know you thought that God was only interested in saving poor little old you—little underprivileged, insignificant you. I know you thought that is all Jesus came to die for. "Oh my," you say, "Jesus could not be interested in any prostitutes or whores. Why would He want to save them? God is not interested in airline executives, movie stars, or other worldly people like them."

I have news for you! Jesus is interested in saving the TV executives and the president of AT&T. He died for those men and He wants them saved. Whether you know it or not, Jesus died for the prostitutes, the whores, the pimps, and the dope pushers. He even died for the Mafia Chieftains. He wants the Godfathers saved.

But you know what? You will never get the attention of people like that with a church rummage sale. The president of one auto maker commands a salary of $900,000 a year. Do you think you can get him interested in coming to a rummage sale? Yet Jesus died for him, and he needs to know it!

We have to present the Gospel in a context that will reach everybody and get their attention, because God is interested in everybody. You will never get a famous movie star, who earns a million dollars for making one picture, to come to a Sunday afternoon church tea fundraiser to get him interested in getting saved. He would not come to something like that. You would have to present the Gospel message in a package that will get his attention, so he can hear the Word of God. Faith comes by hearing and hearing by the Word of God.

Television is one of those packages. But, as I said, it costs big bucks. Through television we can reach people on every level of society, from the lowest to the highest. For instance, it costs $10,000 an hour for air time in some cities, and even more in others. $10,000 an hour! It would take many rummage sales to get $10,000! Ladies, can you imagine baking enough cakes to make $10,000? You would wear your hands out! Then you would be on only one station for one hour. For one year on that station, it would cost over $500,000—a half-million dollars!

Where is that money going to come from? It has to come from the Body of Christ, the children of God.

But how are you going to do it when you do not have five cents, let alone $500,000? How are you going to do it when you cannot pay your bills? You see, the world's system of economics is not designed for you to get ahead. You are beating your head against a wall if you think you will ever get ahead economically in this world. You might as well know that.

Have you ever noticed, after you have walked the picket lines and negotiated for three months, you finally get your demands only to have the cost of living increase and eat up your extra wages? You get a dollar more per hour. Then about two weeks later the price of bread, bacon, and eggs goes up; followed shortly by higher rent and an increase in the cost of gasoline and electricity.

The world's economic system is not designed for you to get ahead. It is designed to keep your nose to the grindstone. What causes the wheels of industry to turn? The fact that you have to go to work. Most people dare not miss a day of work. If they do, it will throw them so far behind economically that they will be six months even getting one nostril above water. They cannot afford to just take off and go to the beach on a beautiful day.

It is all a systematic plan of Satan: Keep men's noses to the grindstone! The sad part about it is most Christians are in the same plight that the rest of the world is in. They owe their souls to the company store. They want to tithe; they want to give to their church and to other ministries, but they cannot. Why? Because they owe everything they make and have to pay it out in monthly payments. Then before they get those bills paid off, something breaks down. With no extra money, they have no choice but to add it to an account. So it keeps going, round and round like a merry-go-round.

You will never be financially independent of the circumstances through your job alone. Yes, we must work. The Bible tells us that. But God has a plan. The

Father has a plan whereby you can become financially and materially independent of the circumstances. That plan is initiated through tithes and offerings.

Once you learn how to operate in God's financial plan, you will reach a point where you have it to give away. You cannot give what you do not have. There is no way. If Satan has his way, you will never get it. But if you will operate in God's plan, you will have it. Once you get to a point where you satisfy all of your own needs, then you will have it to give away. That is when you become effectual as a channel for God to operate through.

Some people have actually reconciled themselves to the idea that they will be working the rest of their lives just like they are now. They do not expect any better. They say, "Well, Grandpa did it that way, and Daddy did it that way, so I guess it is inevitable that I will do it that way, too. When I get to be 65, I will retire." But I am here to tell you that God has a financial plan.

Now I realize that people have been abused and misused. There have been charlatans who have conned people out of their money. No question about it. But the only reason they were able to do it was because the people were not properly instructed. They did not know how to operate in line with the Word of God. They believed the story of any Tom, Dick or Harry who came along and were cheated out of their money.

But there is a legitimate way to operate in God's financial plan. Tithes and offerings are the basis of His plan. I do not know about you, but I am interested in becoming freer than I already am. I want to be so free that I can be a channel, a vessel, that God can use. First of all, I have to get out of my own quagmire of defeatism so I can have something to offer you. If I tried to tell you about financial independence, but was so bound up that I did not have twenty cents for a postage stamp, my message would not be too convincing to you.

You would say, "He is going to tell me to go to church, read the Bible and follow Jesus. Yet he is defeated and whipped. He is scared and can't pay his bills. His family is starving, and he is going to tell *me*? I can't listen to anything he says."

Write a book entitled *Three Ways To Fail In Business* and see how many copies you sell. The books that sell are ones like *How I Took A Hundred Dollars and Made A Million Through Real Estate*. Everybody wants to buy that book.

Nobody wants to know how to lose. You do not have to know how, just stay in bed for a week and you will be a loser. You do not have to study any books on how to lose, just stop going to work for a while and you will be a loser.

People want to know how to succeed, and God has a success plan. I am not talking about some con game. I am talking about material and financial success as a part of the total salvation package that God has to offer. I am not offering financial prosperity and success as the sum total of what Jesus came to do. It is just a part of it, but you have to dissect it in order to talk about it.

We can see this in the medical profession today. Years ago it was the old family doctor who did everything. He took care of general medicine, delivered babies, and treated the horses and cows. He did everything! Today everything is specialized. That is fine, because things aie so complex. A man needs to be a specialist so he can adequately deal with life. Men found that out, so they began to specialize.

We have to take certain subjects out of the total salvation package and examine them under the microscope of spiritual discernment. When I talk about tithes and offerings, that is not the sum total of all that Jesus came to do. It is just a part of it; but it is a vital part, a part that has been underrated over the years. Traditionally, people really have not had adequate and accurate knowledge about it.

We need to realize that prosperity is the will of God. It is God's perfect will that everyone prosper in every area of life. Primarily, we are dealing with material and financial prosperity, because it has to do with tithes and offerings. But it is the will of God for you to prosper. It is not enough for me to say it. You need to know it from a Bible standpoint.

Genesis 12:1-3

Now the LORD had said unto Abram (Abraham), Get thee out of thy country, and from thy kindred, and from thy father's house, unto a land that I will shew thee:

And I will make of thee a great nation, and I will bless thee, and make thy name great; and thou shalt be a blessing:

And I will bless them that bless thee, and curse him that curseth thee: and in thee shall all families of the earth be blessed.

God gave Abraham quite an order. It is quite an inducement to follow God. He said, "I will bless thee and then make thee a blessing." Understand, you cannot be a blessing until you yourself are blessed. This is what God said to Abraham.

Abraham is a representative character. In the New Testament, Abraham is called the "father of the faithful." He was the man God used to get His Word back into the earth realm after Adam and Eve had sinned in the Garden, bringing sin and perdition into the world. Abraham was the channel through which God began a new nation, a new people. Ultimately out of Abraham's loins came Jesus Christ, our Redeemer.

Abraham is always referred to as the father of the faithful. Abraham believed God, and it was accounted to him for righteousness. (James 2:23.) Galatians, chapter 3, verses 13 and 14, says, "That Christ has redeemed us from the curse of the Law, that the blessing of Abraham might come on the Gentiles." So Abraham is a representative character.

Genesis 13:1,2

And Abram (Abraham) went up out of Egypt, he, and his wife, and all that he had, and Lot with him, into the south.

And Abram was very rich in cattle, in silver, and in gold.

Abram was *what*? *Very rich!* It does not say that Abram, or Abraham, was rich. It says he was *very* rich. Then, rather than leave anything to speculation, it tells us what he was rich in. "And Abram was very rich in cattle, in silver, and in gold" (v. 2).

No question about it! Nobody can read human opinions into this and say, "But, Brother Price, he was really referring to spiritual things." That is what somebody always wants to come up with, but the Word of God makes it very plain. You have to be deaf, dumb, blind, or dishonest not to see this. It says: "And Abram was very rich in cattle, in silver, and in gold."

How did Abraham get rich? We could speculate that God made him rich. Or we could speculate that he made himself rich, and God became involved in his life after he was rich. But let us find out from the Bible how he got rich.

Remember, the Bible says God does not change. (Mal. 3:6.) In fact, the Bible says there is not even a shadow of changing (turning) with God. (James 1:17.) He said, "I am the Lord and I change not." Then it is summed up in Hebrews 13:8, relative to Jesus Who is the Son of God and His express image, that He is the same yesterday, today and forever.

So if God made Abraham rich yesterday, He can make us rich today. That is what it is going to take to get the job done. It is going to take the riches of this world, in the hands of the Body of Christ, because *everything* costs money.

Now notice again verse 2 of the 13th chapter of Genesis: "And Abram was very rich (not rich, but *very* rich) in cattle, in silver, and in gold."

Who made Abraham rich? Let us not speculate about it. Let us not take Fred Price's word or anybody

14

else's. Let us read it for ourselves in the Bible.

In Genesis, chapter 24, we find the account of one of Abraham's servants who was sent out to acquire a wife for Abraham's son, Isaac. This man was directed to go to a certain place. When he arrived on the scene, he prayed and asked the Lord to direct him.

> **Genesis 24:29-35**
>
> **And Rebekah had a brother, and his name was Laban: and Laban ran out unto the man, unto the well.** (The servant of Abraham was the man at the well.)
>
> **And it came to pass, when he saw the earring and bracelets upon his sister's hands, and when he heard the words of Rebekah his sister, saying, Thus spake the man unto me; that he came unto the man; and, behold, he stood by the camels at the well.**
>
> **And he said, Come in, thou blessed of the Lord; wherefore standest thou without?** (or outside) **for I have prepared the house, and room for the camels.**
>
> **And the man came into the house: and he undergirded his camels, and gave straw and provender for the camels, and water to wash his feet, and the men's feet that were with him.**
>
> **And there was set meat before him to eat: but he said, I will not eat, until I have told mine errand. And he said, Speak on.**
>
> **And he said, I am Abraham's servant.**
>
> **And the LORD hath blessed my master greatly; and he is become great: and *he*** (referring back to the Lord) **hath given him flocks, and herds, and silver, and gold, and menservants, and maidservants, and camels, and asses** (or donkeys).

Where did Abraham get these possessions? The Lord did it. Now the Bible says God is no respecter of persons. If the Lord made this man great, because he was obedient to the Word of God, will He do less for us? Remember, however, that there are conditions. Abraham followed the Word of God. He obeyed God. True, he made some mistakes, just like all of us, but he always got back in line with God's Word. The Bible says the Lord made him great.

Has God lost His ability to make a man great? Has God lost His ability to prosper a man materially and financially in this world? No! God made Abraham great, and the Bible specifies how the man was made great: God did it.

Some of you are beating your brains out trying to make it in this life. You are working all kinds of schemes and games, trying to get ahead, trying to get rich. Just do it God's way, and He will prosper you just like He did Abraham. He will bless you beyond your wildest dreams and expectations. But you have to do it His way.

We see from these illustrations that God was the One Who made Abraham prosperous in material things. Some of our churches have led us to believe that God is opposed to our having things, but it is not true. Some ministers kept people thinking, "You know, holiness means to be poverty stricken relative to the things of this world." In other words, the fewer things you have is proof positive that you are extremely spiritual. To have material things in this life means you are worldly, not spiritual.

That is how it has been presented to us, but it is not true Biblically! It may be denominationally true. It may be traditionally true. But it is not Biblically true!

Spirituality has nothing to do with what you have or do not have. It has to do with your heart relationship with God. You can be very spiritual and have *nothing* physically or materially. You can be very spiritual and have *everything* physically and materially. Physical and material things are irrelevant to your spirituality. People need to understand that material things will influence and affect your spirituality only if you allow it to.

We used to see certain people in church who were considered spiritual. Someone would say, "That is Brother So-and-so. He is a spiritual man." Poor guy, the bottom of his shoes were worn out and the seat of his pants were worn thin. But he was held up as a paragon of virtue and spirituality.

Another person who drove a nice car or had nice clothes was considered worldly. People would say, "That is Brother So-and-so. You had better watch him. He is very worldly."

People were measuring Brother So-and-so by what they saw. The brother with worn-out clothes may have been a miserly, unforgiving, hard-hearted skinflint, but he was held up as a paragon of virtue simply because he was a man who had very little, materially speaking.

The whole concept of the church world *was*, and still *is* in many places, that spirituality is to be measured by how little a person has of material or worldly things. That is sad. Spirituality has absolutely nothing to do with it, unless you allow it to.

Before we begin to talk about the mechanics of tithes and offerings, we have to know that it is God's will for us to prosper. We have to burst the balloon of tradition that has left Christians with the attitude that it is a lack of spirituality to have possessions of any kind. They have actually missed many blessings that the Father wanted them to have, because they held this mistaken idea: "If I get this, that means I am not spiritual and I want to be spiritual." That kind of thinking will keep you poor. Then when it comes to ministering to the needs of the ministry, you will have nothing to give.

Have you ever been in a meeting when somebody made an appeal for financial support, and the only thing that kept you from giving was the fact that you did not have the money? In your heart you said, "That is a good project, I wish I could give to it, but I do not have a dime."

You had the will to help. You wanted to. But wanting to will not get the job done, just like wanting to pay your telephone bill will not pay it. Your desire to help is not enough. You have to send some money!

I want to say this again, and I want to say it as many times and in as many ways as I can, so you will be sure to understand it: God's financial plan is designed so that you can be a channel for the things of this world to be put into the Kingdom of God. That is the bottom line, the ultimate purpose of it.

In the process, all your needs and desires that are consistent with a godly life will be more than met. Once you get your needs out of the way, you do not have to scramble around trying to pay your bills.

I used to spend hours figuring my money. I never had enough. I would sit up all night with a pen and paper trying to figure out, "How can I meet all these bills?"

I always overbought. It was so easy for me to buy, and I was a sucker just like you. I had no resistance. It always sounded so easy for me to get it. A salesman would boast, "Nothing down, no payment for 45 days. You can handle that. There is nothing to it. Sign right here, Mr. Price."

Then later when I was trying to figure all my bills, a tire would blow out on my car. With no money to buy another tire, the only thing to do was add it to the account.

Then the most embarrassing thing would happen. Maybe you have experienced it. You are standing at the checkout stand with about fifteen people waiting in line behind you. The salesperson says: "The red light on your account has come on. We will have to check upstairs with the credit office." A few minutes later they tell you, "We are sorry. You cannot add anything to your account because you have exceeded your credit limit." It is so embarrassing.

I spent so much time trying to figure how to make ends meet. But you know what? When you have all the ends together, you can do some different figuring: "Father, where should I give this hundred dollars or that thousand?" That is when the fun begins.

Now, praise God, all our bills are paid. But how did we get there? By operating on the principles that

I am sharing with you in this book. And you can get to this same place.

Someone says, "Brother Price, God just blessed you because you are a preacher." That is the dumbest thing anyone could ever say! God did not bless me because I am a preacher.

I was a preacher for seventeen years before I found out about being filled with the Holy Spirit and speaking with other tongues according to Acts 2:4.

I was a preacher for seventeen years before I found out about Mark 11:24 and how to believe God's Word.

If God is blessing me just because I am a preacher, please tell me why God did not bless me during those seventeen years. I was a preacher then.

These things do not work for you because you are a preacher. I can show you lots of preachers who do not have a pot to cook in. You do not get blessed because you are a preacher. You get blessed because you are obedient to the Word of God. Be obedient to God's Word and God will bless you. Knowing what I know now and putting it into operation, I would be blessed whether I was a preacher or not.

Now let me show you that God wants you to prosper. He wants you to prosper in the material area of life. Understand, we are talking primarily about the material area, because we are talking about finances, about tithes and offerings.

In the first Psalm we find further evidence that God wants us to prosper.

Psalm 1:1

Blessed....

That is interesting. The first word out of the Psalmist's mouth is *blessed*! Not cursed, but blessed. The Psalmist starts out with blessings.

Psalm 1:1

Blessed is the man....

This is speaking generically. It covers everybody, both men and women.

I want you to notice, too, that it did not say, "Blessed is the white man." Some people want to use that as an excuse. They say, "Well, you know Christianity is the white man's religion." It did not say, "Blessed is the white man, black man, red man, brown man, or yellow man." It said, "Blessed is the man." That includes me.

Thank God, He did not put any color scheme in there! *Blessed is the man.* That is exciting to me. For too long we have been conned about this color issue. God is color blind!

Some people, who claim to know God, have a color problem. But God does not. He has no color problem. Do you know why God is color blind? Because He does not look at our bodies, He looks at our hearts. Our hearts are the same color because they come from the same factory. Once they have been born by the Holy Ghost, there is only one color: saved!

Psalm 1:1-3

Blessed is the man that walketh not in the counsel of the ungodly, nor standeth in the way of sinners, nor sitteth in the seat of the scornful.

But his delight is in the law (or the word) of the
LORD; and in his law (or word) doth he meditate day
and night.

And he shall be like a tree planted by the rivers of
water, that bringeth forth his fruit in his season; his
leaf also shall not wither; and whatsoever he doeth
shall prosper.

"...whatsoever he doeth..." would have to
include financial security. That means you can invest
money wisely and profit from it.

"...whatsoever he doeth shall *fail*"? No! Prosper!
That means your business will prosper. It means your
health will prosper. It means raising a family will
prosper. Being a wife, being a husband, being a
parent—all that you do will prosper. See what I mean?
He said *whatsoever*. What is the definition of "whatsoever?" It means everything you do.

It is amazing how many people have no prosperity
in their relationships: husbands and wives who cannot stand each other, who hate to be at home. The
woman is standing in the kitchen cooking dinner.
When she hears the car drive up, she says, "Oh, Lord,
he is home again!" That is terrible. It is an awful way
to live. Things are so bad that couples have separate
bedrooms. That is not prosperity!

Parents should be prospering in raising their kids.
But so many parents have no idea where their children
are at night. Their kids go out, and the parents are on
pins and needles until they come home. They cannot
sleep, wondering, "What are they into this time?"

Notice also it does not say "whatsoever *God*
doeth." It says, "whatsoever *he* doeth," *he* being the

man who walks not in the counsel of the ungodly—whatsoever *he* doeth shall prosper.

But wait a minute, there are some conditions to meet.

Blessed is the man that *walketh not in the counsel of the ungodly,* **nor** *standeth in the way of sinners,* **nor** *sitteth in the seat of the scornful.*

But his delight is in the law of the LORD; and in his law doth he meditate day and night.

And he shall be like a tree planted by the rivers of water, that bringeth forth his fruit in his season; his leaf also shall not wither; and whatsoever he doeth shall prosper.

God must want me to prosper. He said that whatsoever I do will prosper. My ministry will prosper because that is what *He* said. That would also have to include finances, so I do not see how prosperity can be an alien gospel as some have claimed.

Let us look at another passage of scripture.

3 John 2

Beloved, I wish above all things that thou mayest prosper and be in health, even as thy soul prospereth.

We see three levels revealed in this verse. "I wish above all things that thou mayest prosper and *be in health...*" Health has to do with your physical body. Then He says, "...even as thy *soul* prospereth." This has to do with the spiritual aspect of your nature.

He says, "I wish above all things that thou mayest *prosper* and *be in health* (physically), even *as thy soul* (spiritually) prospereth." The prospering He first talks about must refer to the only area left: our financial or material life.

Notice this: He does not say, "I wish that thou mayest prosper." No! He says, "I wish *above all things* that thou mayest prosper." In other words, He is saying, "If nothing else happens, I want you to prosper. Above everything else, I wish you to prosper and be in health."

God wants you to be well, even as your soul (the spiritual part of you) prospers. He was saying they already had spiritual prosperity, "even as thy soul prospereth." Then He says, "I wish above all things that thou mayest prosper." That is talking about the material area of life.

God wants us to prosper spiritually, physically, and materially. We are establishing a fact: Prosperity is the will of God; it is the plan and purpose of God.

Whether or not you succeed, whether or not you are prosperous materially or financially, is not based on God. It is not up to God. It is up to you!

This is one thing that has messed up people. They figured, "Well, Lord, I am waiting on You. I am waiting on You to bless me. I am waiting on You to make it work, I am waiting on You to do Your will."

God is saying, "I am waiting on you, child. You do something. I am waiting on you."

It has been a stalemate. We are waiting and God is waiting, so nothing gets done. But I am going to prove to you from the Bible that it is up to you. If you prosper, it is up to you. If you fail, **you** fail. It is **your** problem.

You cannot blame it on God.

You cannot blame it on the white man, the black man, the red man, the brown man, or the yellow man.

You cannot blame it on education or the lack of it.

You cannot blame it on your parents, or where you live, or what side of the tracks you are from.

You cannot blame it on anybody but you!

Do not say, "It cannot be my fault. It is those folks over there. It is their fault. If it was not for them..." No! If it was not for *you*!

You are your biggest problem, not them. You get *you* together, have God on your side, and *them* will not exist. They will not be a problem for you.

In the Book of Joshua, we find further revelation.

Joshua 1:1-8

Now after the death of Moses the servant of the LORD it came to pass, that the LORD spake unto Joshua the son of Nun, Moses' minister, saying,

Moses my servant is dead; now therefore arise, go over this Jordan, thou, and all this people, unto the land which I do give to them, even to the children of Israel.

Every place that the sole of your foot shall tread upon, that have I given unto you, as I said unto Moses.

From the wilderness and this Lebanon even unto the great river, the river Euphrates, all the land of the Hittites, and unto the great sea toward the going down of the sun, shall be your coast.

There shall not any man be able to stand before thee all the days of thy life: as I was with Moses, so I will be with thee: I will not fail thee, nor forsake thee.

Be strong and of a good courage: for unto this people shalt thou divide for an inheritance the land, which I sware unto their fathers to give them.

Only be thou strong and very courageous, that thou mayest observe to do according to all the law, which Moses my servant commanded thee: turn not from it to the right hand or to the left, that thou mayest prosper whithersoever thou goest. (That means wherever you go.)

This book of the law (or the Word of God) shall not depart out of thy mouth; but thou shalt meditate therein day and night, that thou mayest observe to do according to all that is written therein: for then *thou shalt make thy way prosperous,* and then *thou shalt have good success.*

Notice who is going to make the way prosperous: *You!* You are the one who determines whether you succeed or prosper. It is not the man across the street, or the circumstances. **You are the one!**

What God said to this man, Joshua, He says to us. When He spoke to Joshua, it was under the Old Covenant. Praise God, we have a better covenant established upon better promises. To be better means we have everything the Old Covenant had, and then some.

God was saying to Joshua, ''This book of the Law shall not depart out of thy mouth.'' That means you never let what the Word of God says depart from your mouth in the sense of not being there to speak it out. In other words do not fill your mouth with other things; fill it with the Word of God. Why? So that you can speak the Word. Some people will call you a braggart. They will call you everything but a child of God because they do not understand the principle.

That is why I keep saying what the Word says and that is what makes it come. The more I talk about it and say it, the more it comes to me. Why? Because I am putting the power of God to work. How? By faith through the words of my mouth. That is what makes it work.

> ...but thou shalt meditate therein day and night, that thou mayest observe to do according to all that is written therein: for then....

When? When you do what is in the Word.

> ...for then *thou* shalt make thy way prosperous...

Nobody else shall do it but you! You put the Word of God to work, and God will back it up. You are the one who initiates it, the one who puts it into operation. God is the One Who confirms it. Praise the Lord!

2
Locating Your Treasure

The Christian church has not instructed or taught its people relative to many areas of the spiritual life. So there are many misconceptions in these areas. Tithes and offerings is a prime example.

The subject of tithes and offerings has been abused and misused. As a result many people have become "gun shy." When the preacher starts talking about money, they tighten up and say, "Oh, Lord, here he goes. The preacher wants my money." But as I told you in Chapter 1, all you have to do is keep your money in your pocket and the preacher cannot get it.

I will state it again: God has a financial plan, a financial program, for His children to operate under in this life. Under His financial plan you will be blessed coming in and going out. But like any other financial plan, even that which the bank or the savings and loan company may come up with, certain rules and regulations govern its operation. To reap the maximum benefit, you have to operate in context with the plan.

If you want to get the maximum benefit out of a T-bill account, you have to leave your money in the bank, untouched, for six months. You can take it out because it is your money, but you suffer a penalty if you do. To get the maximum benefit, you have to follow the prescribed rules and regulations of the plan.

God has an economic program for His children; and it does not start operating when you get to heaven, it operates in the here and now. Not in the "sweet by-and-by," but in the "sweet now-and-now." The Body of Christ needs to find out how it operates, so it can take advantage of this plan.

God works in the earth realm through men. But for Him to work through men, they have to be in a position for Him to direct them to do certain things. For instance, if God spoke to you and said, "Give that ministry a million dollars," you could not give it unless you had it.

What God has in mind is a financial, economic program to so bless you that all of your needs and desires which are consistent with a godly life will be met. Then you will have such an abundance that you will be a reservoir of finance, a reservoir of material goods. You will be able to take those things and put them into the work of the ministry to promote the Gospel.

But you cannot give away much when your own needs are not met. You cannot do it when you are struggling yourself just to pay your electric bill. So God has a plan that will enable you to be financially and materially independent of the circumstances.

Many people think that spirituality is equated with having none of this world's goods. They have the idea that if you have material things, you lack spiritual vitality, that you are not very spiritual. But as the song so aptly puts it, "It ain't necessarily so." You cannot equate spirituality with material things. It is actually irrelevant and immaterial.

There are many misconceptions concerning God's financial plan in this age. Tithes and offerings are the basis and foundation of the plan. However, before we can get into the mechanics of tithes and offerings— how it all works and how you can get involved in it— we need to establish certain premises.

In Chapter 1 we gave you scriptures to show without doubt that it is God's will for His children to prosper. We showed you Old Testament scriptures and New Testament scriptures. It is these scriptures that I would say epitomizes, or puts into a nutshell, all of the others on the subject of prosperity.

Prosperity is for every Christian. It is God's will that you prosper in everything you do. We need to establish the fact that prosperity is of God. As I said before, some people have the mistaken idea that if you are going to be spiritual and Christian, you cannot have any of this world's goods, because that is a sign of being materialistic or worldly. That is a misconception.

I heard a radio broadcast sometime ago. The preacher was saying: ''Brothers and sisters, do not be deceived. We are not supposed to have material wealth in this life. We are not supposed to have anything. We should expect to have things at the other end. God has a payday coming, but it is not here yet, we will get it at the end.''

Then later he said, ''Now it is okay to get wealth in this life if you give it all away.'' That is a contradiction. I am not knocking the man. I just want to show you that some people believe that way.

31

But you have a choice. You can make up your mind which way to believe. As Joshua said, ''Whom will you serve? But for me and my house we will serve the Lord'' (Josh. 24:15).

Elijah issued the same proclamation. He said, ''If God be God, serve Him. If Baal be God, serve him. How long halt you between two opinions?'' (1 Kings 18:21.) In other words, you can only have one.

You have to make up your mind who you are going to serve, just as you make up your mind what you listen to. You can listen to somebody who says you are not supposed to have anything in this life, or you can listen to the Bible. You cannot find in the Bible what that radio preacher said.

We will now look at Matthew, chapter 6, verses 19-21.

> Lay not up for yourselves treasures upon earth, where moth and rust doth corrupt, and where thieves break through and steal:
>
> But lay up for yourselves treasures in heaven, where neither moth nor rust doth corrupt, and where thieves do not break through and steal:
>
> For where your treasure is, there will your heart be also.

''For where your treasure is, there will your heart be.'' You could turn that around and say, ''Where your heart is, there is your treasure.'' Your heart is your spirit, the inner man, the real you.

Notice again verse 19:

> Lay not up for yourselves treasures upon earth....

Some have misconstrued this verse. They thought Jesus was saying, "You are not supposed to have a savings account or keep any money in the bank." But He was not talking about that. The bank is not even at question here. He was saying, "Where is your heart? Is it in earthly things or in heavenly things?" He was not saying that you should not have money in the bank. He was simply saying, "Where is your heart?"

You can always tell the man whose heart is in money or in the things of this world, because those things become the end in themselves. The acquisition and accumulation of money and things become the reason for his existence. He gets it. He hoards it. He loves it for itself. He is getting it, not to be a blessing to others, but just for the sake of having it. He will never be able to spend it all, but he has millions stashed away while others die without necessities. That is the man whose treasure is laid up on earth, and that is where his heart is.

Jesus tells us to put our treasure where our heart is, and our heart is in the things of God, not in the things of this life. It does not mean that we cannot have the things of this life, or that we should not have them. It means that our heart should not be in those things. Our heart should be in laying up treasures in heaven, not laying up treasures in the bank. But at the same time, that does not mean we cannot have money in the bank.

Do not let your heart be where the money is. Let your heart be in your *heavenly* bank account.

Notice again Matthew 6:19:

Lay not up for yourselves treasures upon earth....

Jesus says do not lay up treasures on earth. Why? Because anything you lay up on earth is subject to earthly conditions, and earthly conditions change.

I remember as a little boy going to the store and with only 10¢ buying enough candy to last for days. In those days you could buy a penny's worth of this and a penny's worth of that. A kid could carry a sack full of goodies out of the store, dragging it behind him, for only about 20¢ or 30¢. You can hardly buy anything for 10¢ now. In some hotel vending machines, soft drinks are 75¢ a can. I remember when you could buy them for a nickel.

The point is that money values change because of world conditions. Almost every day the dollar changes in value. The price of gold is constantly fluctuating, constantly changing. It does not stay even, but always goes up and down, up and down.

The things of the world change. If you put your heart in the things of the world, you will be subject to the conditions of the world. You will be in a bag.

Do not lay up for yourselves treasures on earth, because "...where your treasure is there will your heart be also."

Let your heart be in heavenly things because they are not affected by earthly conditions. It does not matter whether the Democrats or the Republicans are in power. It makes no difference what your bank says or what the savings and loan company says. It does not matter whether the interest rates change or not. The things that are in your heavenly account are not affected by earthly circumstances. They remain the same, and God pays the same dividends all the time.

Remember, we are talking about "tithes and offerings." But in order to talk about tithes and offerings, in terms of the mechanics of their operation, we have to settle some things and establish some parameters. That is what we are doing.

Many people have shyed away from Christianity because of an incorrect presentation down through the years. Some people, especially men, would never go to church because all the church ever did was talk about how you were not supposed to have anything in this life. That is not much of an encouragement, is it?

Somebody was telling me the other day about a girl who gave her testimony. She said that when she was young, her family lived in a ghetto apartment building with twenty apartments on one floor and only one bathroom. Everybody on that floor had to use the same bathroom.

There was another story about people who lived in a place that did not have a floor. In their house the dirt was their floor. That was not in Timbuktu, but right here in America.

Suppose a man comes out of that type of situation. He never had anything in his life. He watched his mother and father struggle; or maybe he did not have a father, but the mother struggled and worked until she finally killed herself. This man made a vow not to live like that. He said, "I am going to rise above that and do better." Then he goes to church and hears, "Do not have anything. Wait until you get over on the other side to get it." He is being told to go right back into the same conditions he came out of.

Jesus never painted that kind of picture. Men, churches, tradition, and theology has, but not Jesus. He never, not once, went with His needs unmet. You cannot find it anywhere in the Gospels. In fact, He was the One Who ended up meeting the needs of other people.

Jesus must have had plenty. He was never caught short. He was responsible for feeding five thousand people at one time. Remember, He had a staff of twelve men who walked with Him every day. They did not work on any job that we have any record of for three and a half years. For that time, He took care of all their transportation, food, lodging, and clothing. He must have had something, somewhere, somehow, or He could not have had a staff of twelve.

The portrayal has been, "If you ever become a Christian, you can forget about using your expertise and ability to do things and make them work in this life." Not really. What you can do is take those things and work them to the glory of God. God needs men like that.

I was privileged to speak at a Kenneth Hagin Campmeeting in Tulsa, Oklahoma, one year when something extraordinary happened. On Thursday night, a special offering was being taken for Rhema Bible Training Center. In fact, all the offerings in the three services that day were going to Rhema's expansion fund.

A man there had gotten hold of the Word of faith and power a few years before through reading Dr. Hagin's book, *The Authority of the Believer*. After finding out how to train the human spirit, he took $500 and parlayed it into assets of over $20 million. Today he is a Spirit-filled, tongue-talking millionaire businessman.

As the offering was being taken, the Lord spoke to his heart. He stood and said, "The Lord has instructed me to match every cash dollar that comes in this offering today." They received about a million dollars. He matched it dollar for dollar.

I wanted to do that too, but I could not, because I did not have a million dollars. That is the purpose of wealth, to promote the Gospel. You cannot take it out and bury it in your backyard, then go out every other night and count it. That is what some people would do if they ever got a million dollars. They could not handle it. They would have security guards around it and everything else, because that is where their heart is.

Give away a million dollars? Why some people would not give God a dollar! In fact, if they do give a dollar, they think they are doing God a favor. Some are so stingy they would not give anything, even when they have it to give.

Some people will never prosper, because their heart is in earthly things. Remember, you do not need very much physically or materially to have your heart in the earth realm and in earthly things.

When you get your heart set right, put it in heavenly things, and learn how to operate in God's financial plan, then you will be blessed and able to be a blessing.

I expect to be a millionaire myself. The only reason I want to be one is so I can have more money to give away. I cannot give away $500,000 if I do not have it, and I want to give it. I know some ministries that could wisely use $500,000. I would like to be a channel of God, because all that God can work through is channels. God cannot drop money out of the sky. Money has to come through the hands of men who are committed to Him.

If you have your minds on the money for the sake of the money and the money becomes the end in itself, it will become distorted and perverted. Your treasure and your heart will become earthbound.

We will now study 1 Timothy, chapter 6, verse 17.

> **Charge them that are rich in this world, that they be not highminded, nor trust in uncertain riches....**

Notice very carefully what this verse *does not* say: "Charge them that are rich in this world *to give away everything they have, so that they can be penniless and poverty-stricken.*" Praise God, it does not say that! Read it again:

> **Charge them that are rich in this world, that they be not highminded, nor trust in uncertain riches....**

"*Trust in uncertain riches.*" That is the issue. Notice the phrase *uncertain riches*. Because of the fluctuation of the world system, whatever you have today can be obsolete tomorrow or of very little value. The dollars today will not buy what it could 25 years ago, so riches are uncertain. They are not good enough to put your heart in. Do not let money or the things of this world be your treasure, because they are uncertain.

Let us look more closely at 1 Timothy 6:17. It is very important. You will be able to see where the Body of Christ has missed some things.

> **Charge them that are rich in this world, that they be not highminded, nor trust in uncertain riches, but in the living God, who giveth us richly all things to enjoy.**

He gives us all things to do what? To enjoy! According to some people, you cannot be a Christian and enjoy anything. To them that only comes after you pass through the pearly gates, in the sweet by-and-by. But that is not what the Bible says.

God wants you to enjoy life. All the things He has given us have been for us to enjoy in this life; but because we did not know it, we have bent everything out of shape. Things have become so distorted and messed up that people do not believe a Christian can enjoy anything. But it is in the Bible. I want us to read the latter part of 1 Timothy 6:17 again:

> **...the living God, who giveth** (not sell or loan it, but giveth) **us richly all things to enjoy.**

Now what could be plainer than that? It is about as plain as the nose on your face. Now look at verse 18.

> **That they do good, that they be rich in good works, ready to distribute, willing to communicate.**

Willing to communicate means willing to give out. This is the key to finding out where a man's treasure is.

Are you ready to distribute? Are you ready to communicate? That is when you find out if you have anything in your heavenly bank account or if it is all in this earthly realm.

You can measure a man's treasure by the commitment to distribute the goods and possessions that fall into his hands. With some it is easy to tell where their treasure is. Some men would not think of giving God as much money as they spend on cigarettes. Some women would not bat an eye at paying $100 or more for a pair of designer shoes. But to them it would be outrageous to put $100 in the offering plate.

You can tell where your heart is. You can tell where your treasure is. Your whole system of values is distorted and perverted if your treasure is in this earthly realm, not in heavenly things.

You need to be ready to distribute and ready to communicate for the purpose of the Gospel. That is how you can measure this. That is why Jesus said, "Lay not up for yourselves treasure on earth...but treasures in heaven." When you have your treasure in heaven, you have a right sense of values.

There is nothing wrong with wearing $100 designer shoes and $300 designer suits. But you ought to be willing to put $300 in the offering plate for the work of the Gospel, and do it hilariously and joyously. Some of your values may be all mixed up. You would pay $15,000 or more for an automobile, but you would not be willing to put $15,000 into the television ministry. You can see the value in that piece of metal, but you cannot see any value in getting the Gospel to the people. You do not see any value in getting souls saved and lives changed by ministering the Word of God to them.

There is nothing wrong with spending $15,000 for a new car by and of itself, so please do not misunderstand me. But you can tell where your treasure is, where your heart is. If your heart is in these earthly things, it is not in the Kingdom of God. If it were in the Kingdom of God, you would be willing and ready to distribute and to communicate. That is how you can measure yourself. That is how you can measure where a man's treasure is, where his heart is.

Where is *your* heart? Is your heart in the Word of God? Is your heart in heavenly things? If it is, you are constantly seeking ways to give, ways to promote the Gospel. Yet, by walking in God's financial plan, you can have the $15,000 automobile, wear the $300 suit, and buy the $100 designer shoes. God does not care. He wants His kids to look good.

It is a matter of getting your priorities right. Matthew 6:33 says, "But seek ye first the kingdom..." It took me some time to see that. I could not think of putting $10 in church. I used to think, "Put $10 in church? Why, that is absolutely unheard of!" But I would buy a tape recorder for $300 and think nothing of it. I would get that $300 tape recorder, put it in my house, stand back, and look at it, thinking, *Wow, look what I have!* But to put $10 in church was like pulling teeth. I would look at my money and say, "$10 in church? Oh, no!" But I paid many dollars for other things. See what I mean? That is how you can tell where your heart is, where your treasure is.

Let us read verse 17 again.

Charge them that are rich in this world, that they be not highminded, nor *trust* in uncertain riches...

41

The danger is in trusting in it. That is what you have to guard against, that you do not start trusting it to be your God, trusting it to be your panacea for all situations. That is where the problems can arise.

There is nothing wrong with riches, because God is rich. If there is something wrong in being rich, then God would not be rich. Does not the Bible say that the earth is the Lord's and the fullness thereof? (Ps. 50:12.) Well, if the earth is God's, then all the gold in the earth belongs to God. So that means He is rich. If it were wrong to be rich, it would be wrong for God to own the earth. Can you see that?

There is nothing wrong in being rich. It is a matter of getting your priorities right. It is a matter of having your treasure where your heart is and having your heart in the right place. Now notice again 1 Timothy 6:17,18:

> Charge them that are rich in this world, that they be not highminded, nor trust in uncertain riches, but (trust) in the living God, who giveth us richly all things to enjoy;
>
> That they do good, that they be rich in good works, ready to distribute, willing to communicate.

Notice the two phrases: *Willing* to communicate and *ready* to distribute. Are you ready and willing? To be willing is one thing, to be ready is another. The main idea of God's financial plan is to put you into a position to be ready. You can be willing, but if you do not have it, you cannot be ready. It is one thing to be willing, but you have to be ready; and you cannot be ready if you do not have it. So you have to get ready before it is going to do anybody any good, especially the Kingdom of God.

Many Christians are willing, but the reason they are willing is because they do not have it and they know that God cannot call on them for it. They do not mind being willing, because they do not have it anyway. They cannot give it, so there is no danger.

But what about those who have it? Are they willing and ready to distribute?

We are establishing the fact of where our heart is, where our treasure is. You see, if God can get a man's heart right, then He has his money. Get a man's heart right and you get everything that belongs to him.

But if your heart is not established right, you will have problems in your life. In Marks' Gospel, chapter 10, verse 17, we see a detailed illustration of this.

Mark 10:17

And when he was gone forth into the way, there came one running, and kneeled to him, and asked him, Good Master, what shall I do that I may inherit eternal life?

Here is a man who came to Jesus, not walking, but running. He did not stand, but knelt and said to Jesus, "What shall I do that I may inherit eternal life?"

Mark 10:18-21

And Jesus said unto him, Why callest thou me good? there is none good but one, that is, God.

Thou knowest the commandments, Do not commit adultery, Do not kill, Do not steal, Do not bear false witness, Defraud not, Honour thy father and mother.

And he answered and said unto him, Master, all these have I observed from my youth.

Then Jesus beholding him loved him, and said unto him, One thing thou lackest....

I want you to see something here. It is amazing that this man came to Jesus and said, "Good Master, what shall I do to inherit eternal life?" Jesus told him, in essence, "Well, do what the commandments say." The man said, "I have always done those things." Then Jesus said, "One thing you lack."

I am here to tell you that this man was in pretty good shape. All Jesus told him was "You only lack one thing." Not a hundred things, just one. In essence, Jesus was saying, "Your game is together. There is just one thing, just one." It is amazing that this man was in such good shape. All that he needed to do was make an adjustment in one area. That is marvelous.

Now let us look at verse 21 again:

Then Jesus beholding him loved him, and said unto him, One thing thou lackest: Go thy way, sell whatsoever thou hast, and give to the poor, and thou shalt have treasure in heaven....

Here we find that treasure in heaven again:

...thou shalt have treasure in heaven: and come, take up the cross, and follow me.
And he was sad...

Now that is something. Jesus was minding His own business, going His own way, when this man interrupted Him. The man came running up to Jesus and knelt down to Him. Jesus did not say to him, "I will tell you how to get eternal life." It was the man who came to Jesus and asked, "What shall I do?"

When Jesus told the man what to do, he was sad about it. That is just the way some people do. I try to tell them how to win and they get sad about it. Now why was the man sad? Verse 22 tells us:

And he was sad at that saying, and went away grieved: for he had great possessions.

I am well persuaded that it was not the intention of the Holy Spirit to say it that way. Literally, it should have read, "Great possessions had him." That is why he could not give them up.

Here is a story that preachers, theologians, Christians, and denominations have totally botched. They have missed the whole point. They think that Jesus was trying to separate the man from his money. They say the man was supposed to go through life not having anything so he would be spiritual. That is not the point of the story at all. The story was about getting the man's heart established in the right place. The Lord Jesus had to get the man's heart where the treasure was and the treasure where his heart was.

That man's heart was not in heavenly treasures, it was in earthly treasures. We know that was the case, because the man could not give them up. Do you know why? Because the possessions had the man. They controlled him. He was dominated by them. The god of money, the god of wealth, the god of materialistic things had this man bound. Mammon is his name. This young man was worshipping at the throne of that God, and it had such a hold on him that he could not give it up. He could not turn loose of those great possessions, not even for eternal life.

You know now where his heart was. His heart was not in heavenly things. He was not laying up treasures in heaven. He did not have great possessions; the great possessions had him.

You may say that someone has a cigarette habit. No, he does not have a cigarette habit, the cigarettes have him. They are dominating and controlling him. If he had them, he could stop. He would not be out of control, he would stop it.

You may say, "That fellow has a drinking problem." No! Drink has him. Drink has him under control. He does not have anything to do with it. If he did, he would stop, especially when he knows it is killing him, tearing up his automobiles, and messing up his marriage. It looks like an intelligent man ought to have enough sense to stop that. He would if he was in control, but he is not.

I can prove that to you with a crude illustration. I use this to shock people into realizing what I am saying. How often do you eat your dinner out of the toilet bowl? You do not eat dinner out of the toilet bowl. (Well, I would hope not anyway!)

Let me make it personal. I do not eat my dinner out of the toilet bowl. Why? Because I am in control. I do not have any problem with that. It is not even a temptation to have dinner in the toilet. I never tell my wife, "Fix the food and bring it to the toilet, we are going to have dinner there tonight."

This sounds crude, but I am not trying to be crude. I am trying to illustrate a truth. The point is, when you are in control of something, there is no problem with it. No problem whatsoever. But where you have a problem, then the problem has you.

Now let us go on, and we will see what Jesus was trying to get to. Jesus did not want this man in the Bible story to be poor. If He had wanted him to be poor, He would also have wanted the man with the $20 million at Campmeeting to be poor. If Jesus had wanted the man in the Bible story to be poor, then He could not have spoken to the man at Campmeeting and told him to match every dollar that was given in the offering for the support of the Bible school, so that more people could be trained in the Word and sent out into the highways and hedges to preach the Word of God. Do you see that?

Jesus had another reason for telling him to give away everything that he had. Jesus perceived that the man's heart was not established in the right place, that the things had him. He had to get the man's heart established rightly, before the man could receive eternal life.

I am well persuaded that if the man had been willing to give it up, Jesus would have said keep it. But in the present state of affairs, He could not afford to tell the man to keep the possessions because the possessions already had control of him. Jesus was trying to separate the man from his false god. Because the man was under control of that god, he went away sad.

Mark 10:21-23

Then Jesus beholding him loved him, and said unto him, One thing thou lackest: go thy way, sell whatsoever thou hast, and give to the poor, and thou shalt have treasure in heaven: and come, take up the cross, and follow me.

And he was sad at that saying, and went away grieved: for he had great possessions.

And Jesus looked round about, and saith unto his disciples, How hardly shall they that have riches enter into the Kingdom of God!

But, Brother Price, did Jesus say that a rich man could not get into the Kingdom?

No, He never said that. He said it was *hard* for them. It is not hard just because they are rich. I have already told you about a man who has over $20 million in assets. It is not hard for him. He is in the Kingdom, giving away millions for the work of the Gospel. He is Spirit-filled, talks in tongues, and lives a clean circumspect life. His family is in line with the Word of God. He enjoys and rejoices in the Word. It was not hard for him to get in.

So what did Jesus mean in verse 23?

...How hardly shall they that have riches enter into the kingdom of God!

Why is that true? Look at verse 24:

And the disciples were astonished at his words. But Jesus answereth again, and saith unto them, Children, how hard is it for them that *trust* in riches to enter into the kingdom of God!

Here is the key: trusting in riches. We read that in 1 Timothy. Paul said, "Tell those that are rich in this world not to trust in uncertain riches." The problem with riches is that you will begin to trust in them. That is where the problem comes in.

The story illustrates this to a tee. That is what happened to the rich young man. He went away. Why? Because his trust was in the riches.

If your trust is in the riches, in the wealth, you will never come out of your financial problems. God will never be able to get involved in your business and money matters, because you do not have your treasure and your heart in the right place. You are laying up for yourself treasures on earth. You are interested in money for the sake of money. You are not interested in distributing to the needs of the Gospel. You are not interested in being a channel that God can speak to and say, "Match all the money in that offering." You are only interested in getting money for yourself, for your own benefit.

That is where it becomes a snare. That is when it can quench your spiritual life and your spiritual development. God is not telling you to be a pauper. He does not want you to be poor. God is not opposed to His children being millionaires. He wants all of us to be rich. There is nothing wrong in that. He is rich. Are we children of a rich Father?

If your heart is not right, then the acquisition of money and wealth becomes an end in itself, instead of a means to the end. What is the end? The end is the proclamation of the Gospel. And in the process, you will get blessed. A hose brings water to you to quench your thirst. Just remember: the inside of the hose gets wet, too! The water has to pass through it.

The wealth that passes through us will bless us at the same time. We should begin to lay up treasures in heaven, not treasures on earth. We should get our hearts set on the things of the Gospel. We need to learn how to operate in God's financial plan so that the acquisition of money and things does not become the end in itself.

We are not to trust in uncertain riches, but in the living God from whom all blessings flow. We should be channels of blessings. God will bless us when we get involved with His plan and learn how to operate through tithes and offerings. Then we will see how to acquire these things to bless us and others at the same time.

3
Heavenly Banking With Tithes and Offerings

Remember, God has a financial and economic plan for His children. It has a twofold purpose. First of all, it is to provide our own material, physical, and financial needs. But it has a secondary purpose equally as important as the first: to finance the proclamation of the Gospel. God wants us to prosper as individuals; and in our prospering, the family of God will prosper.

God has a financial and economic plan for His people, but it is circumscribed by rules and regulations. There are certain laws that govern the operation of God's financial plan. If you do not know what the rules are, if you do not know how they work, and if you do not get in line and in tune with them, they will not work on your behalf.

In Chapters 1 and 2 we have established the fact that God wants us to prosper. He wants us to be prosperous in every area of our lives—spiritually, soulishly, and physically. We also found out where our treasure and our heart should be.

Before finding out how to make deposits in our heavenly bank account, the place where our heart and treasures are located, I want to reinforce the truth about prosperity. The 23rd Psalm is a familiar passage of

Scripture. I imagine it must be one of the most familiar passages in the Bible, along with John 3:16 and the Lord's Prayer. Psalm 23 was one of the first passages of Scripture I learned and memorized when I was saved.

I always thought it had relevancy to the after life. Somehow I thought it had to do with giving me hope for tomorrow, for the future, for "over there" in the Kingdom of God. The churches I went to never gave any intimation that the 23rd Psalm had anything to do with my living right now. But the 23rd Psalm *is* for us now.

However, you can quote it, memorize it, love it, have it framed and hung on the wall of your house, and still go with your needs unmet. I did for years. Though I could quote the 23rd Psalm, I struggled economically and financially. I believed in the 23rd Psalm, but none of it was working for me. None of it had any relevancy to my personal life. Let me show you what I mean.

The 23rd Psalm begins, **The Lord is my shepherd....**

This first statement should alert you to the fact that this psalm is for the New Covenant. In the Gospel of John, Jesus continually talked about Himself as the Good Shepherd. He talked about the children of God, or the family of God, as the sheep. The local assembly, or church, is viewed as a sheepfold.

God sees each individual congregation as a sheepfold—a place where the sheep congregate together to be fed, nurtured, and instructed. Jesus is the Great Shepherd, and He places under-shepherds in each church. He is number one, the boss; then He has an under-shepherd. That is what a pastor is. That is what I am, an under-shepherd under Jesus. The sheep do not belong to me; they belong to the Lord. My job as under-shepherd is to feed the sheep and the lambs. If you feed them properly, you will continually have a new birth of lambs.

Many people have the idea that the preacher or pastor is supposed to go out, get folks saved, and bring them into the church. The preacher is not supposed to do anything like that except as he has opportunities just like you to minister to people and lead them to Christ.

The job of the under-shepherd or pastor is to feed the sheep. The sheep then are supposed to give birth to lambs. You have never heard of a shepherd giving birth to lambs. That is left to the sheep!

Notice how personal Psalm 23 is. The Lord is not *our* Shepherd; the Lord is *my* Shepherd. You have to see this as speaking to you as an individual, which it is. It does not say the Lord is *our* Shepherd because He might not be yours. You might not see Him as that. But I need to see Him as Shepherd if I am going to get any benefit, as each one of us should.

Psalm 23:1 could have said only, "The Lord is my shepherd." It could have put a period there and gone on to the next verse. But the next clause is very interesting. It almost seems as if there is no need to say it, because it has nothing to do with Him being our

53

Shepherd; yet He sticks it in. I believe it has much relevancy. It is for us today.

Psalm 23:1

The Lord is my shepherd; I shall not want.

Philippians 4:19 says, "My God shall supply all your need according to his riches in glory by Christ Jesus." If all my needs are met, then I will not have any wants or needs. Yet think of the many Christians whose needs are not met. They go day after day, week after week, month after month, year after year, as I did with my needs never really being met.

To me every day was a struggle. The next week was a struggle. The next month was a struggle. As I looked down the years, every year was a struggle, because I could only see the coming years as the present was. The present was bad, so the future looked bad.

That is why some people commit suicide. They look at today and today looks so dismal, so bad, and without any hope. They look at tomorrow, and tomorrow looks just like today. They look at next week, and next week looks just like today. They look at next month, and next month looks just like today. They look at next year, the next five years, the next ten years, and they say, "What is the point in going on? Every day is going to be just like today. I might as well end it now."

The Psalmist said, "The Lord is my shepherd; I shall not want." I memorized this, I quoted it, I loved it; yet I was in want. God is not a liar. If He said I shall not want, then if I am in want, I must be missing something. If He lied about that, He may have lied about the whole thing. We may as well throw away the Bible, close down the church, and go on our own merry way.

"The Lord is my shepherd; I shall not want." If I shall not want, that means all my needs will be met. Yet I was going with my needs unmet. My whole life was a struggle economically and materially. And that is where we live our lives.

You are a spirit, but you live in a physical body. It is your physical body that drives physical cars, wears physical shoes, eats physical food, and sleeps in physical beds. You cannot talk about the spirit without talking about the physical, because that is where you live your spirit life—in the physical. When your physical is not doing too well, it will affect your spirit.

Psalm 23:1,2

The Lord *is* (present tense) my shepherd; I shall not want.

He maketh me to lie down in green pastures: he leadeth me beside the still waters.

There are many things in this psalm that I will not cover in this book. I just want to show you some things relative to tithes and offerings which have to do with God's financial plan and His provisions for us in a material and financial way.

Verses 3,4

He restoreth my soul: he leadeth me in the paths of righteousness for his name's sake.

Yea, though I walk through the valley of the shadow of death, I will fear no evil...

Why? Because God has not given us the spirit of
fear, but of love and of power and of a sound mind.
(2 Tim. 1:7.)

Verse 4 continues:

**...I will fear no evil: for thou art with me; thy rod and
thy staff they comfort me.**

Notice, we are talking about bringing this into the
present and making it relevant to where we are *now*.

Verse 5

Thou preparest a table before me...

Notice that it is not me who has to *provide* the table,
and it is not me who has to *prepare* the table. It is God.
The Psalmist says, **Thou preparest**. Not after a while
or by and by, but now. It is in the continuous present
tense. It does not say God *will* prepare, it does not say
God *has* prepared.

Verse 5

**Thou *preparest* a table before me in the presence of
mine enemies....**

That dates this psalm and lets us know when it
is to be in operation.

Thou preparest a table before me (or in front of me)
in the presence of mine enemies....

"In the presence of" means that while God is
preparing the table, the enemy is standing around
watching. That could not be heaven. It could not be
after a while, by and by. There will be no enemies in
heaven.

God is preparing the table in the presence, not in
the absence, of the enemy. The enemy cannot do any-

thing about God preparing the table, but he can do something about your partaking of the table. That is where we have been defeated. That is where we have been wiped out. The enemy cannot stop God from preparing the table; but if we allow it, he can keep us from eating from the table. If he can trick us and keep us from partaking of the table, it is the same as wiping out the table. It might as well not be there if I am not getting any benefit from it.

The table will be set. Where? In the presence. Of whom? The enemy. So that could not be talking about heaven. There will be no enemies in heaven. There will only be relatives, friends, angels, the Father, Jesus, and the Holy Spirit.

Verse 5

...thou anointest my head with oil....

This is another proof that it is talking about the time in which we are living. This is the age of the Holy Spirit. The Holy Spirit was poured out or given on the Day of Pentecost. We are in the age of the Holy Spirit. Oil in the Scriptures is a type of the anointing of the Holy Spirit, the empowering of the Holy Spirit.

...thou anointest my head with oil; my cup runneth over.

My cup does not have just a few drops in the bottom. *It runneth over!*

Notice it does not say, "My cup *shall* run over." It does not say, "My cup *ran* over." It says, "My cup *runneth* over." That is in the continuous present tense.

If my cup is running over, that means I have an abundant supply. More than enough. It means I have enough for somebody else to have some. My cup is more than full. It is running over.

We do not have to live on "Barely Get Along Street" down the block next to "Grumble Alley." We ought to have plenty. God said our cup runs over.

Can you see how we have been deceived? We have thought that in order to be spiritual, we had to barely make it and just have enough. No way!

Your cup ought to be running over right now! Is it? If not, then you are not operating in God's financial plan. You are not taking advantage of your covenant rights.

Some people, who are mercenary in their objectives, will try to do these things for no other reason than to gain the material benefits. Let me say emphatically, if your motives are not right, it will not work!

There are people who are not interested in following the Word of God. They are not interested in being a channel of blessing to others. They are not interested in following the Lord Jesus Christ all the way. They are only interested in getting their hands on some material things. They like to hear about prosperity, because all they are interested in is getting some money.

You do not operate in God's financial plan in order to get things. You do it because you love the Lord, because you want to be faithful in every area of life, because you want to be a good steward of the things of God. You do not do it for what you can get out of it personally; you do it because you love Him. Yet in doing these things for Him, you *will* gain personally. This is a part of it.

When I first entered into the life of faith and the power of the Holy Spirit, I did not know a person could be blessed materially and financially. I did not get into this faith life because of that, but because I found out how to live in peace and be an overcomer in life instead of a victim of the circumstances. I had no idea that it had anything to do with material things or that it could do anything about causing money to come my way.

I saw it in God's Word, so I said, "Hey, this is how to walk with God." I wanted to be obedient. I wanted to follow the Lord and be a faithful messenger of God. I wanted to hear Him say at the end of the way, "Well done, thou good and faithful servant." That was my only motive.

It was not until *after* I entered in that I learned how my God would supply all my need according to His riches in glory by Christ Jesus. I learned then that the cattle on a thousand hills belong to God; and because they belong to Him, they belong to me.

I did not start walking in faith because of what I could get out of it. I had found a way that I could finally please God by walking in line with His Word. Instead of being a "doubting Thomas," I could be a "believing Fred." Praise God!

Then I found out about all the fringe benefits. I said, "He made it available to me. He must want me to have it." I began to see that it was a total life-style, covering every aspect of life. God wanted me to be blessed and to be a blessing. Well, I could not be a blessing until I was blessed. I had to find out how to get blessed in order to be a blessing.

I believe the 23rd Psalm clearly shows us that these things are for us now. We do not have to want. We can operate in the fullness of God and have a cup that is running over. It is a blessing to walk in the fullness of God and be a channel of blessing to others. We can walk above the clouds instead of having to walk in them, trying to figure out where we are going.

Jesus said lay not up for yourselves treasures on earth, but treasures in heaven. In essence, we have a heavenly bank account. I want to ask you a question. Do you know how much money you have in your checking account or savings account? You should! Do you know how much you have in your heavenly bank account?

You cannot make withdrawals, either from your earthly bank account or from your heavenly bank account, unless you have made deposits. Many are trying to make withdrawals from God without ever having put anything in the bank.

Some have had the idea that God was some great big Santa Claus, some cosmic bellhop that they could run all over the universe at their whim. They thought that by saying, "Father, I need this," He would run and hand it to them.

God is not some kind of magic wand. He works by divine order and divine principles. I struggled for years materially and financially, but remained at the bottom of the heap. Then when I found out how to walk in line with God's Word, His divine order and principles, I began to rise to the top. Now, like the Word says, I am blessed going out and blessed coming in.

Somebody will always say, "Yes, but the reason you are blessed like that is because you are a preacher." Friend, I was a preacher for 17 years and had nothing but a hard way to go. Why should I be getting things now because I am a preacher? I am no more a preacher today than I was for 17 years. I was not getting blessed before. All I got then was the short end of a big stick.

It is not a matter of being or not being a preacher; it is a matter of getting in line with the program—operating according to divine rules, and giving God a channel through which He can bring to pass those blessings in my life. I was not doing that before. Now I am; and because I am, I am being blessed—and I will be blessed even more. The blessed is going to get blessed.

I am not blessed because I am a preacher. I know many preachers who do not have a thing. One reason I know that is because so many are always coming to me, asking for something. I know many preachers who are literally struggling. I used to be one of them.

I am blessed because I have learned how to walk in line with God's Word—and I know many other people who have done the same thing. For instance, the man I told you about earlier in this book, who has $20 million or more in assets. He is not a preacher. How did he get blessed? Why is God blessing him? Because he learned how to walk in line with the Word of God. He is a successful businessman, not a preacher.

In order to make withdrawals from your heavenly bank account, you have to learn to make deposits. It is a spiritual transaction, yet it comes back in a material way. It is both spiritual and material. If your need is in the material realm, then you receive in the material realm. If your need is in the spiritual realm, then you receive in the spiritual realm.

We have a heavenly bank account, but we have to know how to make deposits. The reason many people have problems with their heavenly economics is because they are having problems with their earthly economics. If you cannot reconcile your earthly checkbook and keep your earthly savings account in line, you will not be able to keep your heavenly bank account in line.

That is why I asked if you know how much you have in your heavenly bank account. How can you make a withdrawal if you do not know what you have in there? It is impossible to make a withdrawal from a bank in which you have no money deposited. In fact, you cannot get money out of your own bank account if you do not have enough in it to cover the check you have written. That check will bounce. It does not make any difference whether or not you have an account if it is insufficient funds.

Some people have not learned how to take care of their business spiritually any more than they have learned how to take care of their business economically.

Even at our church account, we receive checks returned from the bank. In 99% of the cases, they are marked "Insufficient Funds." That means there is not enough money in the bank. What an indictment against Christians, against Spirit-filled believers!

If you write a check when there is not enough money in the bank to cover it, you are actually lying. What a witness that is to the people at the bank!

Why are checks returned marked "Insufficient Funds"? *Most* of the time it is because that person does not know what he has in the bank. He does not reconcile his checkbook. Do you think banks send you cancelled checks for the fun of it? They are for your benefit. You are supposed to take those checks and reconcile your checkbook to be sure you have what the bank says you have.

Some people just keep on writing checks. They never record their checks and deduct them. When they get their monthly statement showing that they have $875 in the bank, they look at it and say, "I have $875. That is wonderful! I can go out and write some more checks!" They do not realize that there are some outstanding checks that have not cleared the bank yet. They really may have only a few dollars in the bank. Then when they write more checks, those checks bounce.

The point I am making is that spiritual things are closely akin to physical things. I know how much I have on deposit in my heavenly bank account, just like I know how much I have in my regular checking account. I make it a point to know. Then when I ask the Lord for something, I know I have enough on deposit to cover it.

Your heavenly Father will give you your return. It will come so supernaturally and so quickly sometimes that it will stun you. But you have to be consistent in making deposits into your heavenly account, just as you do in your earthly bank account.

There are two primary ways to make deposits into your heavenly bank account. The first way is tithing. The second way is offerings—also called giving to or investing in the Gospel. "Tithes and offerings" is the subject we will deal with. We are going to get into the mechanics of tithes and offerings shortly, but now we are laying a foundation.

Tithes and offerings is how you make deposits into your heavenly bank account. If you have not received anything, it is because you have not given anything. You are not getting anything, and you never will.

It is not a matter of God penalizing you. He is not standing over you, saying, "You did not give me anything, so I am not going to give you anything. I will fix you!"

It is a matter of divine laws and principles, just like your earthly bank. If you do not put any money into the bank, how can you earn interest on it? The bank is not penalizing you. You did not invest anything. You did not put anything into the account. How can you draw interest on something you did not deposit? It is not a matter of God trying to mistreat you because you did not give Him anything. It is not "an eye for an eye and a tooth for a tooth." No! God *cannot* do anything because you have not done anything.

Somebody says, "Yes, Brother Price, but tithing is under the Old Covenant. It is under the Law." No! Tithing did not originate with the Law. Many traditions are really not according to the Word of God; but we have to deal with them first before we can get down to the nitty-gritty.

Many people have misconceptions. They say, "Well, I am not going to tithe. I cannot see any sense in tithing. That was under the Law." No, it was not *under* the Law in terms of its *originating with* the Law.

Tithing has always been God's universal financial principle. It has always worked, and it will work until there is no further need for it to work. It is God's method or way of providing sustenance for His children—for their own personal needs—and then, of course, for the needs of the Gospel.

You see, we are to be stewards of the things of God. We are to be channels of blessings, because God works through human channels.

God can only work through the hands that are available to Him, and the hands can only do what they are capable of doing. If they do not *have* anything, they cannot *be* anything, *give* anything, or *do* anything. We must have it first in order to give it. If God directs you to put some money into a ministry, you cannot do it if you do not have it.

Have you been in a church service or a convention when an appeal went forth that you wanted to contribute to, but could not because you did not have the money? You had the will, but you cannot pay bills with will and your good intentions will not accomplish a thing.

As I said before, tithing did not originate with the Law of Moses. We can see this fact revealed in Genesis, chapter 14.

Genesis 14:13-20

And there came one that had escaped, and told Abram the Hebrew; for he dwelt in the plain of Mamre the Amorite, brother of Eshcol, and brother of Aner: and these were confederate with Abram.

And when Abram heard that his brother was taken captive, he armed his trained servants, born in his own house, three hundred and eighteen, and pursued them unto Dan.

And he divided himself against them, he and his servants, by night, and smote them, and pursued them unto Hobah, which is on the left hand of Damascus.

And he brought back all the goods, and also brought again his brother Lot, and his goods, and the women also, and the people.

And the king of Sodom went out to meet him after his return from the slaughter of Chedorlaomer, and of the kings that were with him, at the valley of Shaveh, which is the king's dale.

And Melchizedek king of Salem brought forth bread and wine: and he was the priest of the most high God.

And he blessed him, and said, Blessed be Abram of the most high God, possessor of heaven and earth:

And blessed be the most high God, which hath delivered thine enemies into thy hand. And he (Abram) gave him tithes of all.

In verse 20 we see the first mention of the word *tithes*. Abraham gave Melchizedek tithes of all. Whether you are aware of it or not, chronologically speaking, this event happened approximately 430 years *before* the Law was given to Moses at Mount Sinai.

People were aware of tithes before the Law ever came into existence. So it is incorrect to say, "Tithing is under the Law," meaning it originated with the Law. Tithing was incorporated into the Law because tithes and offerings are God's methods of blessing His people, financially and materially, and He wanted Israel to be blessed. But tithing did not originate with the Law.

In the 28th chapter of Genesis, we have a follow-up to what we just read in the 14th chapter about tithes. Tithing is Biblical. It was used under the Old Testament Law, but it did not originate with the Old Testament Law.

Genesis 28:10-14

And Jacob went out from Beersheba, and went toward Haran.

And he lighted upon a certain place, and tarried there all night, because the sun was set; and he took of the stones of that place, and put them for his pillows, and lay down in that place to sleep.

And he dreamed, and behold a ladder set up on the earth, and the top of it reached to heaven: and behold the angels of God ascending and descending on it.

And, behold, the LORD stood above it, and said, I am the LORD God of Abraham thy father, and the God of Isaac: the land whereon thou liest, to thee will I give it, and to thy seed;

And thy seed shall be as the dust of the earth, and thou shalt spread abroad to the west, and to the east, and to the north, and to the south: and in thee and in thy seed shall all the families of the earth be blessed.

Remember this is exactly what God had said to Abraham. Isaac and Jacob came out of the loins of Abraham. What God had said to Abraham would come to pass through Isaac and Jacob.

Now let's continue in Genesis, chapter 28:

Genesis 28:15-22

And, behold, I am with thee, and will keep thee in all places whither thou goest, and will bring thee again into this land; for I will not leave thee, until I have done that which I have spoken to thee of.

And Jacob awaked out of his sleep, and he said, Surely the LORD is in this place; and I knew it not.

And he was afraid, and said, How dreadful is this place! this is none other but the house of God, and this is the gate of heaven.

And Jacob rose up early in the morning, and took the stone that he had put for his pillows, and set it up for a pillar, and poured oil upon the top of it.

And he called the name of that place Bethel: but the name of that city was called Luz at the first.

And Jacob vowed a vow, saying, If God will be with me, and will keep me in this way that I go, and will give me bread to eat, and raiment to put on,

So that I come again to my father's house in peace; then shall the LORD be my God:

And this stone, which I have set for a pillar, shall be God's house: and of all that thou shalt give me I will surely give the tenth unto thee.

A tithe is a tenth. The word *tithe* means one tenth. If it is not a tenth, it is not a tithe.

This incident also happened before the Law was given. The Bible says in the mouth of two or three witnesses, let every word be established. (Matt. 18:16.) We have given you two and have shown in each case that tithing was a known and practiced way of life before the Law of Moses was given. Abraham and Jacob tithed.

Tithing is God's primary way of materially and financially blessing His people. If you say, ''I cannot afford to tithe,'' I can only say, *you cannot afford not to.*

4

Procedures For Bringing the Tithe

God has, as I have said before, a financial plan for His people. That plan is supposed to operate within the framework of the Body of Christ, the Church. When I say "the Church," I do not mean buildings or denominations. The people of God are the Church.

The plan has a twofold purpose: (1) to provide all of the material and temporal needs of God's people, and (2) to promote and spread the Gospel throughout the world, or in other words to finance the proclamation of the Gospel.

God's financial and economic plan operates under very strict rules, just like banks or savings and loan institutions. If you do not conform to a bank's rules, requirements, and regulations, you will not be allowed to handle its money for your benefit and purposes. But if you meet all of a bank's requirements, it will advance you the funds.

We have shown you very clearly from God's Word that it is the will of God that His children prosper, that they be prosperous in every way.

We showed you from the Word of God that we have a heavenly bank account. Jesus told us about laying up treasures in heaven. There are ways to make deposits into that heavenly bank account and also ways to make withdrawals.

We told you that the two basic ways of making deposits are tithes and offerings.

In the last chapter, we showed you from the Bible that tithing did not originate with the Law. Tithing is for the New Testament Church. We will find out more about that as we go along.

In the 26th chapter of Deuteronomy, we have an illustration or outline of the procedures for tithing. We are not talking about the mechanics of tithing—what tithing is—but rather how to bring them. There is a procedure, a Biblical admonition, as to how we ought to bring our tithes to the Lord.

Deuteronomy 26:1

And it shall be, when thou art come in unto the land which the LORD thy God giveth thee for an inheritance, and possessest it, and dwellest therein....

We have presented to our view the fact that God had a land, an inheritance, a possession for His people. God is telling them what they are to do when they come into their possession. Notice again what He says:

And it shall be, when thou art come in unto the land which the LORD thy God giveth thee for an inheritance, and possessest it, and dwellest therein....

Remember that this is referring to the children of Israel, who were to come into a material, physical land—a land that flowed with milk and honey. It was to be their homeland, their dwelling place, where they would spend their lives.

Whether you realize it or not, God has a land for His children now. I do not mean when we die and go to heaven. I am talking about in the here and now. God promised Israel a physical land, because they were physical people. But we are both physical and spiritual.

Colossians 1:13

Who hath delivered us from the power (authority and dominion) **of darkness, and hath translated us into the kingdom of his dear Son....**

Every born-again Christian has been translated into a land or kingdom. We are in the Kingdom of God *now* if we are Christians.

Now we need to make a qualification. If you read through the Gospels, you will notice (in the Gospel of Matthew particularly) the emphasis placed on the use of the words "kingdom of heaven." Over and over again, you will hear Jesus making reference to the Kingdom of Heaven. On the other hand, when you read the Gospel of John, you will see another phrase, "the kingdom of God." Many Christians have the idea that the Kingdom of Heaven and the Kingdom of God are two different ways of talking about the same thing. But I submit to you that they are not the same.

The Kingdom of Heaven is future; it has not yet come. The Kingdom of Heaven will operate in this physical earth and will be a political system. It will be a theocracy, *theos* meaning God. It will be a God-ruled government through a prime minister or king, Jesus Christ. He will be the agent of the Kingdom in the earth realm. It is future and has not come yet.

Why is it called the Kingdom of Heaven? Simply because its place of origin is heaven. It does not originate in the earth realm like the Democratic and Republican parties, dictatorships, or the Communist

Party. The origin of the Kingdom of Heaven is heaven, but it will operate in the earth realm. It is a God-ruled political system, a theocracy.

When you go to the store and buy an article, many times you will find stamped on it the words "Made in Hong Kong" or "Made in Japan." What does that mean? It means that its place of origin was Japan, Taiwan, or Hong Kong.

"Kingdom of Heaven" simply means its place of origin is heaven. The Kingdom of God, on the other hand, is a present tense reality in the earth realm today. The way you get into the Kingdom of God, which automatically gives you entrance into the Kingdom of Heaven when it comes, is by way of the New Birth.

John's Gospel, the 3rd chapter, records Jesus talking to the man Nicodemus and saying to him, "...except a man be born again, he cannot enter into the Kingdom of God."

What is the Kingdom of God? It is God's reign and rule in the entire universe, physically and spiritually. When we receive Christ as our personal Savior, we enter into the Kingdom of God. We become citizens of that Kingdom. In that Kingdom we have the dominion, authority, and power of Almighty God to be victors over the circumstances of life. That Kingdom flows with milk and honey.

Notice again what it says in Colossians 1:13.

Who hath delivered us from the power (authority or dominion) **of darkness, and hath translated us into the kingdom....**

We are in the Kingdom of God right now, and we have the authority of the Name of Jesus. We have the Word of God and a New Covenant that provides everything for us over and above what the Israelites had when they entered into the Promised Land. God said when they came into the land to possess it that there was something to do.

If we have received Christ as our personal Savior, we are in the Kingdom of God right now. We are not yet functioning in the Kingdom of Heaven, because that has not come. We are still in the earth realm, under man's government. But the day will come when all of that will be done away with, and God will come down and govern through Jesus Christ. That will be the Kingdom of Heaven. In the meantime, we are in the Kingdom of God. We are in the Promised Land right now.

Many people have thought that the Promised Land was when we go to heaven. I used to think that when I heard the saints of God singing:

> *On Jordan's stormy bank I stand,*
> *and cast a wistful eye*
> *Into Canaan's fair and happy land*
> *where my possessions lie.*
>
> *I am bound for the Promised Land...*
> *I am bound for the Promised Land...*
> *Who will come and go with me?*
> *I am bound for the Promised Land.*

I am here to tell you, we are *in* the Promised Land! The Kingdom of God is *now*. Not when you die. Not after a while. The Promised Land is the reign and rule of God through the Holy Spirit, which is the day of grace that we are in now. It is the Kingdom of God and is entered by the New Birth. You become heir to all of the benefits and privileges of that Kingdom. We are in it now because the Word says so. Remember:

Colossians 1:13

Who hath delivered us from the power (authority and dominion) **of darkness, and hath translated us into the kingdom....**

Now let us look at something else.

Deuteronomy 26:2,3

That thou shalt take of the first of all the fruit of the earth, which thou shalt bring of thy land that the LORD thy God giveth thee, and shalt put it in a basket, and shalt go unto the place which the LORD thy God shall choose to place his name there.

And thou shalt go unto the priest that shall be in those days, and say unto him, I profess this day unto the LORD thy God, that I am come unto the country which the LORD sware unto our fathers for to give us.

Notice the first part of the 2nd verse again:

That thou shalt take of the first of all the fruit of the earth....

Remember, Israel was primarily an agrarian society. The people basically were farmers and cattle-men. They did not go to the factory and punch a time clock. The things that they had to offer were their crops and cattle. This was the sweat of their brow.

But, you see, in a mechanized metropolitan society like most of us live in today, the sweat of our brow brings us the dollar. That is the fruit of our labor. You go to work and beat a typewriter or do some other job all day long. Then at the end of the week you get a paycheck. That is your fruit. The dollar is the fruit of your labor. That is what we have to bring to the Lord as the fruit of our labor.

The Israelites could not punch time clocks. The fruit of their labor came out of the ground basically. Notice again Deuteronomy 26:2:

> ...thou shalt take of the first of all the fruit of the earth (Notice He says the *first part*, not the last, not the second, but the first.), which thou shalt bring of thy land that the LORD thy God giveth thee, and shalt put it in a basket, and shalt go unto the place which the LORD thy God shall choose to place his name....

Crenshaw Christian Center, which I pastor, is one of those places. God raised up this ministry, not man. Your church may be one of the places, too.

Deuteronomy 26:3

And thou shalt go unto the priest that shall be in those days, and say unto him, I profess....

We are in the Kingdom right now and, whether you know it or not, we have a priest in this Kingdom and in this land that we are in. Let us find out about our priest.

Remember, God told the people to bring their first-fruits in a basket unto the priest of those days and say, or profess, unto Him. Now Hebrews 3:1 says:

> **Wherefore, holy brethren** (that is us), **partakers of the heavenly calling, consider the Apostle and High Priest of our profession, Christ Jesus....**

You have a High Priest—not your pastor or any other ministry gift, but Jesus. Jesus is your Priest.

What do you think Jesus has been doing for the 2,000 years since He went back to heaven? Have you ever thought about it? What does Jesus do every day? What has Jesus been doing while we have been working and living? He has been interceding on our behalf. He is our Priest, ministering in the heavenly sanctuary on our behalf.

Remember in the 26th chapter of Deuteronomy, God said to the people, "...when you come into the land, take your firstfruits...." That is talking about your tithes. The tithe comes right off the top. That is your firstfruit. "...Take your firstfruits, put it in a basket, and bring it to the place where I shall choose to place My name...." Then He said, "...Bring it to the priest of those days and profess this before that priest."

I want to emphasize that Jesus is our Priest. We have read one verse that said, "Consider the Apostle and High Priest of our profession, Jesus Christ." Then in Hebrews, chapter 6, we have further revelation.

Hebrews 6:17

Wherein God, willing more abundantly to shew unto the heirs of promise (us) the immutability of his counsel....

Immutability means that He does not change. In Him there is no variableness or shadow of turning.

Hebrews 6:17-20

...the immutability of his counsel, confirmed it by an oath:

That by two immutable things, in which it was impossible for God to lie, we might have a strong consolation, who have fled for refuge to lay hold upon the hope set before us:

Which hope we have as an anchor of the soul, both sure and stedfast, and which entereth into that within the veil;

Whither the forerunner is for us entered, even Jesus, made an high priest for ever after the order of Melchisedec.

Hebrews 7:1-8

For this Melchisedec, king of Salem, priest of the most high God, who met Abraham returning from the slaughter of the kings, and blessed him;

To whom also Abraham gave a tenth part (or a tithe) of all; first being by interpretation King of righteousness, and after that also King of Salem, which is, King of peace;

Without father, without mother, without descent, having neither beginning of days, nor end of life; but made like unto the Son of God; abideth a priest continually.

Now consider how great this man was, unto whom even the patriarch Abraham gave the tenth (or a tithe) of the spoils.

And verily they that are of the sons of Levi, who receive the office of the priesthood, have a commandment to take tithes of the people according to the law, that is, of their brethren, though they come out of the loins of Abraham:

But he whose descent is not counted from them received tithes of Abraham, and blessed him that had the promises.

And without all contradiction the less is blessed of the better.

And *here* men that die receive tithes; but *there* he receiveth them, of whom it is witnessed that he liveth.

When it says, "...**here** men who die receive tithes...," it is talking about the ministers of God, such as the pastors. We receive your tithes and offer them up to God. But we are going to die. "And **here** men that die receive tithes; but **there** he receiveth them...." If you read through the whole context, you will see that this is referring to Jesus. It is talking about both a physical and a spiritual truth. He is making an analogy between Abraham and Melchisedec, and Jesus and us.

What did Jesus Christ tell John when He appeared to him on the Island of Patmos? John saw Jesus and heard Him say, "I am he that liveth, and was dead; but behold, I am alive for evermore..." (Rev. 1:18). That is what He is talking about here in Hebrews 7:8.

> **...but there he receiveth them, of whom it is witnessed that he liveth.**

That is why when we bring our tithes and offerings, we offer them up to Jesus. He is the priest of these days. We should confess, or profess, unto Him that we have come into the land, into the country. We are in the Kingdom right now.

We will now go back to the 26th chapter of Deuteronomy and look at the third verse again:

"And thou shalt go unto the priest that shall be **in those days**...." Jesus is the Priest of these days, meaning our day.

"...and **say** unto him...." We should not just throw our offering into the offering bucket. We should open our mouths and say something. Say what?

"...say unto him, **I profess**...." In other words, confess. Say it with your mouth. *What* do you say?

"...I profess this day unto the Lord thy God, that **I am come....**"

He did not tell us to say, "Well, someday after a while, I will finally make it. If I can just hold out until the end, I will make it." No! He said, "Say unto Him I *have* come." That means, "I am in it now."

Our profession or confession should be: "Father, we are in Your Kingdom now. We are in the land that You have given to us. We have inherited it, and we are possessing it. We are receiving the milk and honey blessings."

Deuteronomy 26:3 again:

And thou shalt go unto the priest that shall be in those days, and say unto him, I profess this day unto the LORD thy God, that I am come unto the country which the LORD sware unto our fathers for to give us.

Deuteronomy 26:4

And the priest shall take the basket out of thine hand, and set it down before the altar of the LORD thy God.

That is what Jesus is doing. That is what He does when you give your tithes and offerings. He receives them. He takes them and sets them before the altar in the high sanctuary of heaven.

Deuteronomy 26:5

And thou shalt *speak* and *say* before the LORD thy God....

This is the profession:

Deuteronomy 26:5-10

And thou shalt speak and say before the LORD thy God, A Syrian ready to perish was my father, and he went down into Egypt, and sojourned there with a

few, and became there a nation, great, mighty, and populous:

And the Egyptians evil entreated us, and afflicted us, and laid upon us hard bondage:

And when we cried unto the LORD God of our fathers, the LORD heard our voice, and looked on our affliction, and our labour, and our oppression:

And the LORD brought us forth out of Egypt with a mighty hand, and with an outstretched arm, and with great terribleness, and with signs, and with wonders:

And he hath brought us into this place, and hath given us this land, even a land that floweth with milk and honey.

And now, behold, I have brought the firstfruits of the land, which thou, O LORD, hast given me. And thou shalt set it before the LORD thy God, and worship before the LORD thy God.

This was their profession, their confession. Israel looked back to their origin, back to their bondage. They said to the Lord, "Out of Egypt You brought us."

They related how they had started out with one man, Abraham. Out of Abraham came Isaac, and out of Isaac came Jacob. Jacob had twelve sons and eleven of them sold the twelfth, Joseph, into Egyptian bondage. God preserved Joseph in Egypt. When the famine came into the land, Joseph had found favor with Pharaoh. As a result, Jacob's family went down into Egypt and became a great nation.

Then Satan, through a pharaoh that did not know Joseph, decided that he was going to stop the Israelites from multiplying; so he brought hard bondage and taskmasters upon Israel. But the Israelites cried out to

God and God sent Moses to deliver them. Moses led them through the Red Sea, across the wilderness, to the banks of the Jordan River. Across the river was the Promised Land. Finally after forty years Joshua and Caleb led the children of Israel into the Promised Land.

Through this profession, they were relating these things. They were saying, ''We remember how we started out. We came through bondage, hard trials, and tribulation. We remember that You heard our cry and delivered us.''

When they brought their tithes and offerings, they looked back and made a confession. They looked back to Egyptian bondage, but then they traced their history from that bondage to their present place where they stood in the Promised Land, and they proclaimed the blessing and gave praise unto God.

Now, *we* have entered into the Kingdom. Satan had us bound. He had us in bondage. He had our lives bound up in sin, but Jesus came and set us free so we could enter into the Kingdom of God.

How did we do it? Through Calvary. In our profession, we go back and look at Calvary, because that was the place where our redemption began. That is what we profess when we come before God.

We declare that we are in the land that flows with milk and honey. It flows with the blessings of God, with all the things that are needful, desirable, and consistent with a godly life—things that will put us on top in every circumstance. We have that right now.

When we bring our tithes and offerings, we should expect to lay them before our High Priest, Jesus

Christ, knowing He will go before God the Father and make an offering before Him on our behalf. When we come, we ought to confess (profess) and praise the Lord for it.

Now we are going to make a confession. I want to give you an illustration of the kind of confession you can make in this Kingdom Age. Here is an illustration:

> Heavenly Father, we profess this day to You that we have come into the inheritance which You swore to give us. We are in the land which You have provided for us in Jesus Christ.
>
> We were sinners serving Satan; he was our God. But we called upon the Name of Jesus, and You heard our cry. You delivered us from the power and authority of darkness and translated us into the Kingdom of Your dear Son.
>
> Jesus, as our Lord and High Priest, we bring to You the firstfruits of our income that You may worship the Lord our God with them.
>
> Father, we rejoice in all the good which You have given to us and to our household. We have heard Your voice and have done according to all You have commanded us.
>
> Now, Father, look down from Your holy habitation in heaven and bless us as You said in Your Word. Father, we believe that we now receive Your blessings according to Your Word. This is our confession of faith, in Jesus' Name.

This is the kind of profession you can make to the Lord your God when you bring your tithes. That is the procedure to bring it.

Question: "How long should we make this profession or confession?"

84

Hebrews 10:23 tells us:

Let us hold fast the profession of our faith without wavering; (for he is faithful that promised;).

"To hold fast" means to hold tight and do not let go. In other words, we should make this profession all the time.

Whenever we come before the Lord with our tithes and offerings, we should come before Him, making a profession of faith. We should declare that we are in the Kingdom, that we have come into the land that flows with milk and honey. In our spirits we ought to see Jesus taking our tithes and offerings and going before our heavenly Father and worshipping Him with them. Then we should look up and see the smile of the heavenly Father as He receives the obedient offerings of His children.

You might think God just wants you to do this so He can have something. Just remember, He does not need anything you have. There is nothing your money can do for God. He was God before you were created or ever thought of. He was God before this earth was made. In fact, He has a city with streets made out of gold. How many streets in your neighborhood are paved with gold?

When God asks you to bring the tithe and offering, it is not for His benefit, it is for *your* benefit. We bring it to Him. Then He through us is able to take it, multiply it, and use it to bring blessings to others.

5
Why Bring the Tithe?

Malachi 3:10

Bring ye all the tithes into the storehouse....

Notice it says, "all the tithes," not a part of the tithes.

"Well, Brother Price, I put a little over here and a little over there."

It does not say to do that. It says, "Bring **all** the tithes into the storehouse."

Notice it says *bring* the tithes, not *send* the tithes.

A person said to me, "Brother Price, I am going to move to another state. But I get fed here. I will be watching the television ministry and getting the tapes. I want to send my tithes to Crenshaw. How am I going to bring my tithes every week from New York to Los Angeles? I would be spending $500 round trip for air fare to bring a $50 tithe."

You have to understand that there may be extenuating circumstances which would negate your being able to physically bring your tithes. In a case like that, common sense would dictate that you mail the tithes and save the $500 air fare.

The idea is that if you are able to bring it, you have no excuse not to. Unless you do not have a car, have no friends or relatives who own cars, the buses have stopped running, and the taxi cabs are on strike, then you ought to bring your tithes into the storehouse, because that is what God said. Besides that, it is coupled with the New Testament injunction: "Not forsaking the assembling of yourselves together, as the manner of some is..." (Heb. 10:25).

So bring your tithes. If there is an extenuating circumstance, such as a geographical situation, it would be permissible to mail it or send it with someone else. But if you do not have a legitimate reason for not bringing it, then you are out of line with the Word if you do not bring it. Fair enough?

Bring ye all the tithes into the storehouse, that there may be meat in mine house....

"The storehouse" is God's house, not man's house. It is the place set aside for the worship and praise of God, the place from which the Word of God should go forth to feed the people.

Each local church or assembly is actually a sheepfold. The pastors are under-shepherds—shepherds under Jesus, the Great Shepherd. The sheep (Christians) gather to be fed. The local church *should* be a storehouse, a place where the Word is stored so that those who need the Word can come into that storehouse and receive what they need to nourish them spiritually. It takes money to establish and maintain the storehouse. If the storehouse does not minister to the needs of the people, then it is surely not a place where God has placed His Name. God puts His Name where His Word is, where the sheep can be fed. In Malachi 3:10, He goes on to say:

Bring ye all the tithes into the storehouse, that there may be meat in mine house, and prove me....

Here is a very important point. God actually challenges man to prove Him. It is a very unusual situation when God challenges man. Usually you will hear this (perhaps you have said it yourself), "I am not going to believe in a God I cannot see. I do not believe in that religious stuff. It is a bunch of junk. Tell you what...if God will show me a sign, then I will believe." Or, "If God will do this, then I will do that." In other words, the responsibility is always placed on God's shoulders. He has to make the first move.

But here is a place where God gets the jump on us. He challenges us. The beautiful thing about this is that God in His infinite mercy, love, and knowledge knew that in the day and time in which we live, the dollar would mean everything to people. People will say, "You can take my goldfish and my cat, but leave my money, honey! Do not bother my green stuff!" People will sell their souls for a dollar.

God knew the great emphasis that would be placed on economics in this world. So He challenges us in the area that is closest to most people, their money. So the play is ours. We have the ball. There is the goal line. It is up to us to run for the touchdown. Notice again what it says:

Bring ye all the tithes into the storehouse, that there may be meat in mine house, and prove me....

You do it. **You** prove Him. He has given you the way to do it: by tithes and offerings, by your money. He challenges you by saying:

Bring ye all the tithes into the storehouse, that there
may be meat in mine house, and prove me now
herewith, saith the LORD of hosts, if I will not open
you the windows of heaven....

Notice the word "windows." It is in the plural,
not the singular. It does not say "window"; it says
"windows."

Read the account in Genesis concerning the Flood.
It says the fountains of the deep were broken up and
the *windows* of heaven were opened. It rained for forty
days and forty nights, flooding the whole earth. That
same kind of "flood" is referred to here in Malachi.
God will open the *windows* of heaven! What an
experience—to be flooded with $10 bills, to go swim-
ming in a lake of $10 bills! But that is what He said:

...prove me now herewith, if I will not open you the
windows of heaven, and pour you out a blessing, (not
a curse, but a blessing!) that there shall not be room
enough to receive it.

It will not be just enough to keep the bill collector
off your back. It will not be just enough to see you
through until you can sit down and figure out how you
can "rob Peter to pay Paul."

He said there would not be enough room to
receive it. That has to mean abundance! More than
enough!

Now it is up to you to prove Him. How are you
going to do it? Notice it says, "Bring ye all the tithes,"
so you have to *give* first. If you really want to find out
if it is true, there is only one way: Bring all the tithes
into the storehouse and prove Him.

You may have thought the preacher was just trying to get your money, but that was not true. Now I agree that there have been misuses and abuses relative to tithes and offerings, but that is no reason—no legitimate reason—for you to say, "Well, I ain't gonna give and let that preacher get all my money." To prevent that, as I have already told you, keep it in your pocket and nobody will get it. You cannot use that as an excuse.

Yes, there have been abuses and misuses, but I am not going to stop giving, just because some preacher pulled a trick and people were dumb enough to fall for it.

I have been to some churches and seen the preachers operate. Then I thought, "Those dumb people, if they are so stupid to do what that ding-a-ling said, then they ought to lose their money, their shirt, their shoes, and everything else!"

Some preacher stands in front of the pulpit with one of those giant Bibles in his hands. Then he opens it and says, "Now all of you who really love the Lord, all of you who really believe, bring your money down here and put it on top of this Bible." Anyone who would fall for some dumb trick like that ought to lose all his money! That is not God's way.

Yes, there have been abuses—I will be the first to admit it—but there have also been abuses in relationships between parents and children. Are you going to stop being a parent just because there have been some bad parents?

There have been some bad husbands. Are you going to stop being a husband just because some other husband did not do right?

There have been some bad wives. Are you going to stop being a wife just because there are some bad wives?

Some ladies have had bad experiences with men. Maybe you have, too. Because "Mr. Tall, Dark, and Handsome" came by and tricked you, your attitude now is: "I don't want anything to do with a man! There ain't no good men, they're all just dogs!" You just lied. You are reading after a good man right now. Ask my wife and children. You will find that I am a good man. I am not perfect, but I am a good man. I intend to be good and I am working on being good.

You cannot use as a cop-out that all men are no good. That is a lie, just like some men, who have been tricked by women, saying, "There ain't no good women! They're all alike!" No, they are not. I have a good one.

So do not glibly say, "All the preacher wants is my money," just because some preacher tricked you out of yours. That is no reason for you not to tithe and give offerings. God says, "Prove Me." He challenges you to prove Him.

Atheists say there is no God, and agnostics are not really sure. This is how they can find out once and for always. Do what God said. Prove Him and see if He will not open to you the windows of heaven and pour you out a blessing. He said there will not be enough room to receive it.

> **Bring ye all the tithes into the storehouse, that there may be meat in mine house, and prove me now herewith, saith the LORD of hosts, if I will not open you the windows of heaven, and pour you out a blessing, that there shall not be room enough to receive it.**

I can tell you that is true. God's blessings are uncountable. I am not talking about pie-in-the-sky after a while. I am talking about in this life. He said, "I will pour you out a blessing, and there will not be enough room for you to receive it." Not only that, but we have it here in the Word that God will actually get involved with the enemy (Satan) who would try to destroy you.

Let us read the last clause of the 10th verse and move right into verse 11:

> **...and pour you out a blessing that there shall not be room enough to receive it. And....**

"And" means that is not the end of the thought. God is not through talking yet. He is still talking basically on the same subject. He says:

> **And *I* will....**

My goodness, *you* will not have to do anything once you bring your tithes. You can just sit back and watch God clobber the devil for you in this area. Look at what He says:

> **And I will rebuke the devourer for your sakes....**

God said He will do it for you, but only *relative to tithes*. In every other instance, *you* have to do it. You have to take your authority, your spiritual authority, in the Name of Jesus.

The Bible says in James 4:7, "Resist the devil, and he will flee from you." Ephesians 4:27 says, "Neither give place to the devil." Mark 16:17 says, "In my name cast him out." Luke 10:19 says, "Walk on him." He said, "I will rebuke the devourer for your sakes."

Whether you know it or not, there is a devourer loose in this earth realm. He seeks whom he may devour, and he does not care who it is. Male or female, young or old, smart or dumb, ugly or pretty, tall or short, black or white—it does not make any difference to him. He is out to get you! It ought to be obvious by looking at the world around you.

There is a force loose in the earth realm that seeks to drive men into the ground, to spoil them, destroy them and make them miserable in every way. That force is Satan. God said that if you bring the tithes, "I will rebuke the devourer for your sakes." Then look at this:

> **And I will rebuke the devourer for your sakes, and he shall not destroy the fruits of your ground.**

Glory to God! That means you will be successful. It means your business does not have to fail. It means that all you set your hand to will prosper. It means that if you plant crops, your crops will grow even if everybody else's die.

God said He would rebuke the devourer and He will not destroy the fruit of your ground. I believe that means in every area of life for the Christian, whether male or female. I believe that a Christian woman need never worry about having a miscarriage. She should not have any complications in the delivery of her child.

And I will rebuke the devourer for your sakes, and he shall not destroy the fruits of your ground; neither shall your vine cast her fruit before the time in the field, saith the LORD of hosts.

In those days God was talking about an agrarian society, basically farmers and sheepherders. It is different today, but the principle still remains. Today it has to do with monies and the things that you have invested, because that is the fruit of your labor. You have invested it and it should come back to you. It should not fail.

Remember though, God said it is only *relative to tithes.* He said, "I will do it—I will get involved. I will rebuke the devourer for your sakes, *if* you will bring the tithes."

Just think, you are going to hit the enemy from two sides. God is going to clobber him on one side, and you will be walking on him, rebuking him, and casting him out on the other side! How can you lose? There is nothing for you but to win!

Notice that all of this is predicated upon your proving God. The way you prove Him is to tithe. *You* have to tithe. That is a part of God's economic program, a part of His financial plan.

Believe me when I tell you it works. I cannot describe to you how well it works. It works so well until sometimes I am tempted (though I do not yield to the temptation) to be embarrassed about being blessed—I am so blessed. I have done what God said. I have proven His Word. I took Him at His Word—not so that I could get blessed, but because I love Him. I did it out of obedience to His Word. I did it because I have control over what happens to my money. I am the one who decides where my money goes.

Because of my love for Him and my desire to be obedient, I started out by doing what His Word says. I have so many deposits in my heavenly bank account that the withdrawals are coming out of my ears. I am blessed! **I am blessed! I AM BLESSED!** The Word declares it, and I am blessed!

I taught this one morning at our eight o'clock church service. When I had finished teaching and was greeting the people at the front of the church, a man walked up to me, shook hands, and put a piece of paper in my hand. It was a $10 bill. Another man came up, shook hands, and gave me a piece of paper folded up. I put it in my pocket and later found it to be a nice crisp brand new $100 bill. That happens to me all the time.

"Well, that just happened to you because you are a preacher." Is that so? I was a preacher for 17 years before I ever came into the knowledge of what I am sharing with you.

Would you please tell me why God did not bless me during those first 17 years? Nobody *ever* gave me a $100 bill during those 17 years, and I was just as much a preacher then as I am now. Why was I not getting any blessings then? If you get it just because you are a preacher, why are so many preachers camped on my doorstep, trying to get a handout from me? Why are they not being blessed?

I do not receive these blessings because I am a preacher; I get blessed because I live in line with the Word of God.

What did God say in Malachi 3:10? He said, ''I will open the windows of heaven and pour you out a blessing that you will not have enough room to receive.''

God is not going to drop that blessing out of the sky. It is going to come through the hands of men in some way, by some form or fashion. It will be God speaking to people. I did not tell those people to give me that money, but I received it in Jesus' name and agreed with them for the one hundredfold return on it.

That happens to me all the time now, but it never used to—never! I could not beg, borrow, or steal it. During those 17 years there was never enough. But I found out how to get involved in God's financial plan, how to do what the Word says.

I remember when I first heard about tithing many years ago. I was a brand new Christian, just saved. I was not brought up in what is called a Christian home. I did not go to church until after I was married. I did not know anything about church as such. What little I did know was what I had heard, and most of that was negative.

We joined a church where the preacher was always coming up with some kind of scheme to get the people's money. He started talking about tithing. He really did not teach on it like I am teaching now. He did not go into any detail about it, but he mentioned enough to put people under condemnation if they did not tithe. It made you feel guilty if you really wanted to obey God.

As a baby Christian, I wanted to do anything and everything I could to please my heavenly Father. I was so glad that He had not cast me out, that He loved me in spite of myself and He saved me though I did not deserve it. I wanted to be obedient and tithing was something I could do, because I was in control of my money.

We really could not afford it, but I wanted to tithe. I wanted to be obedient, so we tithed. We tithed for quite a while and never received a thing. *Windows?* We did not get one window, not even the little window in the closet, opened for us. We tithed for a long time, but there was no significant change in our economic situation.

Now why? God is not a liar. He says in the Word, "Bring the tithes into the storehouse, and I will open the windows of heaven and pour you out a blessing that there will not be enough room to receive it." That never happened to us though we had tithed for a long time. It was a struggle to tithe, but I wanted to do it because I wanted to be obedient to God.

We had many hard trials and tribulations, economically speaking, and could not figure out why. It was not until many years later that I came into the knowledge of God's Word. I found out that there is a spiritual warfare going on out there. We are involved with spiritual beings that desire to destroy us, to steal from us, and extract from us anything beneficial. It is Satan, the devourer, that God said *He* would rebuke. He said, "I will rebuke him for your sakes."

You see, Satan operates like a highwayman. Have you ever seen any of the old cowboy movies? The robbers would cover their faces with bandannas and wait in the bushes until the stagecoach came. Then they would ride out and start chasing the stagecoach. Bang! Bang! Bang! They would stop the coach, take the strongbox, and ride off with it. In other words, they would rob the stage.

In John, chapter 10, verse 10, Jesus said, referring to Satan, "The thief cometh not, but for to kill, steal, and destroy." Satan is a robber, a highwayman.

Remember that all of your blessings start out in the spirit world. By an act of your faith, the blessing which starts out in the spirit world is manifested in the physical world as a material commodity. Here is what Satan does: He has his henchmen—his angels and demons—waiting in the bushes. You are sending your tithes up, making your deposit in your heavenly bank account. But you do not realize that you have to use your faith *with* your tithing or else Satan will steal your blessings.

God is not a liar. If you bring all your tithes into the storehouse, He will open the windows of heaven and pour you out a blessing. The moment you put your tithes in, the return starts on its way from God. However, while it is coming down from the spirit world into the physical world—into the town where you live—Satan's henchmen are waiting at the edge of town to waylay the stage and steal your blessing. So you are tithing, but nothing is coming back. You do not realize that the devil was waiting to steal every bit of it, and there is nothing God can do about it. It is up to you whether or not the devil steals from you.

Now understand, God said He would rebuke the devourer, but even there you have to use your faith or the devil will take advantage of you and steal from you. A lack of faith on your part will tie God's hands. God cannot act on your behalf if you are not operating in faith.

All those years that we tithed, we did not get anything for it. We were being obedient to the Word, but we did not get the windows-of-heaven blessings. We did not realize that the blessings were coming, just like God said, but Satan was waiting at the edge of town robbing the stage and stealing all that belonged to us. We were trying to figure out, "How come it is not coming?" The churches I went to did not tell me anything about that.

The devil stole from me until I realized what was happening. He has not stolen from me since. I do not allow it any longer. My blessings are coming in all the time. I am bringing in the tithes. In other words, I am putting so much seed into the ground that I cannot do anything but get a harvest. It is coming in all the time, everyday. Every time I turn around, more is coming in—and more will always be coming in. I have made it a point to invest much into the Kingdom through tithes and offerings. I know how to use my faith, so Satan cannot stop my blessings from coming.

I am sure there are many Christians who have known about tithing for years and probably even tithed, but never really had much change in their personal economic situation. Do you know why? Because they did not understand how to operate in faith.

When you give your tithes, you still have to believe God for the return. The windows of heaven will be opened and God will pour the blessings out, but He never said *you would get it.*

That is a very important point of distinction. If you do not know how to operate in faith, you *will not* get the blessings. Even though God is pouring it out, the devil will steal it, just like he will steal your health, your job, or anything else. You have to use your faith to stand against him. You have to take the Word of God and claim your rights.

Every time I give, I say, "Father, in the Name of Jesus, I believe that I receive the windows-of-heaven blessings. Satan, take your hands off my money!" Then he cannot touch it.

Before I did that, Satan was stealing everything and I did not even know it; I thought it was God. I said, "Maybe He does not want me to have it this time," but I found out that He *does* want us to have it. If you do not get it, you cannot give it; and if you cannot give it, the Gospel will not be spread throughout the world.

You have to bring the tithe, place it in the storehouse, then confess the return on it. You should confess in the Name of Jesus: "I believe I receive the windows-of-heaven blessings; and I thank You, Father, for rebuking the devourer for my sake. I thank You that his hands are tied concerning my money." Then the devil cannot touch your money. You have to see your return coming to you by faith.

Now realize we are talking about only one facet of the Christian life, so do not get upset. Do not be like some who have come to our church and criticized saying that all I talk about is money.

I am trying to teach people how to be blessed, how to take advantage of all that God has made available to them. I found out how to do it, and I am sharing it with you at no cost. Everything we do costs money, so you had better know how to get it. You are being charged higher prices these days for everything, so you had better learn how to increase your income, so you can not only keep up, but go above that and have a supply to give into the Kingdom of God. You cannot give what you do not have. Do not wait until Satan has you up against the wall. Start laying up treasures now.

It is unfortunate but true that most of us, when we first heard about how to walk by faith, how to be filled with the Holy Spirit, and about tithes and offerings were already embroiled in problems. In fact, it may have been your problems that allowed God to get your attention. You were going your merry way, skipping through life, ignoring God and everybody else. When times got hard, there was no one else to look to.

God did not cause your hard times. God had been calling you, but you could not hear Him because of the loud disco music. Have you ever had that happen? Maybe you were listening to some music or had the radio up full blast. When you turned it off, you heard the telephone ringing. It did not suddenly start ringing. It had been ringing for a while, but you could not hear it because the music was so loud.

That is what happens so many times in people's lives. They are so involved doing their own thing that they do not hear God calling them. God is calling you all the time. In fact, He starts calling you at the cradle and never stops until you enter the gates of hell (unless you receive Jesus). He is always calling you. When you first heard Him is not when He first started calling you—that was just when you stopped and listened.

When I came into this knowledge of God's financial plan, I was so in debt—I owed my soul to the company store! Do you know what I am talking about? Though I have said it before, it bears repetition, because there are people who can relate to this. Talk about holding your head above water—I barely had one nostril above the water! It was just that bad financially. When I heard about this, I owed everything. In fact, for a while my kids did not even belong to me! I owed the doctor and the hospital, and I could not pay for them. The hospital held the pink slip on my kids! I was just the registered owner!

It was terrible!

My life was so messed up. Like so many other people, I ended up playing catch-up, trying to overcome the deficits of the past. If I had known 25 years ago what I know today, I would not be waiting to be a millionaire. I would be one so that I could have it to give away. I cannot give it if I do not have it. I want to give, but I can only give what I have. In order to give it, I have to get it.

Start using your faith today. Start operating in the principles of the Word right now. Do not wait until you can tithe $500. Tithe the $10 you have right now. You have to start out in the things of God and then grow with them. Start using your faith in the area of finances.

I did this in 1970 when I first saw it in the Word. I did not get into it because of the financial blessings or because of material things. I got into it because I thought it was the will of God for me to be free. All I wanted was to be obedient and be free in my own life. In fact, I really did not know about all of the fringe benefits: of being well and not having to be sick; of being wealthy and not having to be poor. In those days I was just happy to know that I was filled with the Spirit and could walk in the love of God and be pleasing in His sight. It was after I got into the Word that I found out about all the fringe benefits. I did not start doing it, *trying* to get something by doing it. I started doing it because I saw it was right.

I wanted to be obedient to the Spirit of God and to the Word of God—then I saw that there were blessings attached to it. I found out that there were some fringe benefits connected to the contract. So I thought, *There is no point in my missing out on the fringe benefits. I might as well have the contract and the fringe benefits.* That is when I started cashing in on them.

Even though we were financially strapped, I began to tithe on what I had. I began to say, "I believe I receive the windows-of-heaven blessings." Like it says in Ecclesiastes 11:1, I began to cast my bread upon the waters. The writer said I would find it after many days. He did not say I would see it fifteen minutes later or even the next morning. He said, "Cast thy bread upon the waters and thou shalt find it after *many days.*" So I kept throwing that bread out there.

It was several years before we saw any appreciable change in our financial situation. But down in my spirit, in my heart, I formed an image of financial freedom. For the first time in my life, I saw myself with money in my pocket. I saw myself able to give.

Oh, how many times I had been to a meeting where an appeal was made for financial support of some work of the Gospel. I saw it to be an honest work and wanted to make a contribution, but I did not have anything to give. I said, "Oh, the day will come when they make an appeal and I will be able to give! I will be able to share! Praise God!" I saw that in my spirit. I saw all of the bills paid. I saw myself free. I began to say, "I believe I receive the windows-of-heaven blessings."

I kept putting that bread out there. Jesus said, "Give, and it shall be given unto you; good measure, pressed down, and shaken together, and running over" (Luke 6:38). I just kept at it.

Then slowly but surely, it started coming in, a little here and a little there. It got bigger and bigger until finally it became a tidal wave. Oh my goodness, it knocked me down and ran right over me! I said, "Go ahead, Lord, knock me over again! Hit me again!"

I had so much that I was able to pay off everybody and give some away. Before, I was always trying to figure out, "What bill am I going to pay this time? I sure can't pay them all!" All of a sudden I could ask, "Where am I going to give *this* money? What ministry am I going to give to this time?" Talk about joy unspeakable and full of glory! It really gets to be fun when you can give it away. But I started out with a little at a time.

You see, if you cannot believe God to heal a headache, forget about believing Him to heal cancer. If you cannot handle a headache with your faith, how are you going to handle cancer? Do not wait until the doctor says your case is terminal before trying to get healed. Start using your faith on the little issues of life. Believe God instead of taking an aspirin.

I have never heard it said (unless there were some other complications associated with it) that headaches are terminal. I have never heard of people dropping dead from an ordinary headache. The worst that can happen is your head will hurt. Instead of taking a pill, use your faith. I am not saying it is wrong to take a pill. Do not let anyone put you in bondage about that. Learn how to stand against a headache. If you cannot stand against a headache, you will never stand against a coronary—never. Your faith will not have been developed.

When the next headache comes around, start using your faith instead of taking a pill. Learn how to eradicate headaches with your faith.

Begin to use your faith to believe God for shoe strings. Soon you will be able to believe for shoes to go with the strings.

Begin to use your faith. Do not wait until you get to the end of the road. Do not wait until the doctor says there is no hope—*no hope!* If you do, you will not be coming to God in faith; you will be coming to Him in desperation, and it will not work.

That is why when so many Christians die, people say, ''The Lord took him. It was the Lord's will.'' No! His faith was not sufficiently developed to handle that attack from the enemy. He was not coming in faith anyway at that point; he was coming in desperation. He would have grabbed onto a straw if you had thrown it to him.

The same principle works in giving as it does in the other illustrations I have given you. Bring your tithes. Start using your faith and believe God for the return on your giving. All you can hope to receive are the windows-of-heaven blessings.

6
Are You A God Robber?

Malachi 3:8

Will a man rob God? Yet ye have robbed me. But ye say, Wherein have we robbed thee? (And God answers:) **In tithes and offerings.**

God is asking a question: *Will a man rob God?* The answer is either yes or no. Will a man rob God? That means woman too.

I wonder, are *you* a God robber?

Will a man rob God? (That is a good question.) **Yet ye have robbed me.**

This is not the preacher speaking. It is not the church, or Fred Price. This is God saying: *...Yet ye have robbed me.*

That is a heavy indictment. God said, "You have robbed me."

The people say, "Wherein have we robbed you?"

God says, "In tithes and offerings."

Based on what I see in this verse, this is my opinion: If I am not a tither, I am a God robber. That is what the Bible says: If you are not a tither, you are a God robber. *I* did not say it; *God* said it. If you are not a tither, you are a God robber.

Are *you* a God robber?

I am glad I can say, "I am not a God robber." I *was*! For years, I robbed God without realizing it. But when I robbed God, I was also robbing myself! I was the one getting cheated, because God is still God, whether I give Him anything or not. My giving to Him does not make Him God. He *is* God whether I give Him anything or not.

He said, "Will a man rob God?" That is a good question—one that we need to deal with. He says:

...But ye say, Wherein have we robbed thee? In tithes and offerings.

Now notice, *God* asks, "Will a man rob God?"

Then the people ask, "Wherein have we robbed thee?"

God answers, "In tithes and offerings. Ye are cursed with a curse: for ye have robbed me, even this whole nation."

Whether you know it or not, there is a curse loose in this earth realm. There are multitudes of people operating in that curse without even knowing it. I operated in that curse for years and did not know it. The devil had me, a black man, thinking the man next door who had white skin and blue eyes was my problem. He also had the man with the white skin and blue eyes thinking that the black man was his problem. While we were arguing and fussing back and forth, the devil was stealing from both of us.

I honestly used to think that the problem was my black skin. All the black people that I knew, in the circles in which I ran, had the short end of a very big stick. To me it looked like the white people had all the blessings. It seemed as though they had all of what we call "this world's goods."

People just do not realize that everybody has the same problems. The only difference is our problems are on different levels. For instance, you can look at a millionaire and say, "He does not know what I am going through. He does not have any problems." But you see, he has problems that you do not have. For instance, who are his friends? He does not know whether people like him or his money. So he has a bigger problem than you ever thought about having. After all, the people hanging around him may be leeches, trying to get his money.

I never will forget an article I read several years ago. It was a personal interview with one of the richest men who ever lived. In that interview it was revealed that this man had been married several times. He said, "I would give half of my money, my possessions, my fortune, if I could have one successful marriage." That is tragic. It would seem that if he had all that money, he would never have any problems.

Here is a man who has the money to buy a whole herd of cows, have them specially butchered for him, and then prepared to eat just the way he wants. Yet he is so scared somebody is going to steal his money that he has an ulcer eating away his insides. All the man can have for dinner is *Half & Half* and raw eggs! You think you have problems? Your problem is that you cannot buy the steak. Here is a man who can buy the steak but cannot eat it. It is the same problem only on a different level.

I used to think that my problem was somebody else. I thought *they* were trying to keep things from me. Do not misunderstand me. I am not so naive that I do not realize that there are individual people who do not like me. There are some black folks who do not like me and there are some preachers who do not like me, so we know it is not just a matter of color. But we have been conditioned to think that was the case.

My friend, I found out that it does not make any difference what color you are. If you learn how to operate within the context of God's financial plan, there is no one on the face of this earth—white, black, red, brown, or yellow—who can keep your blessings from you. The thing I did not know was that I was operating in that curse. Notice again what God said in Malachi 3, verse 9:

Ye are cursed with a curse.

Did you know it is a curse not to have enough money? Being unable to provide for your family and going with your needs unmet is a curse. I lived in that curse for years without knowing it and never had enough.

The devil would lie to me and say, "See that man down the street? He is your problem." Then I would get mad at the man. But that man was not my problem. He had his own problems.

I thought that way until I found out how to operate in the power of God's Word. I honestly did not know that curse was out there. Nobody told me.

The curse started when Adam sinned in the Garden of Eden. When Adam sinned and disobeyed

God, he opened the door and allowed the curse to enter into the earth realm. Ever since that happened, men have lived in poverty and fear. They have been cheating, killing and stealing from one another—all because of the curse that came because of the sin of Adam.

But God planned a way to overcome that curse through His Son Jesus Christ, by faith in His Word and by operating in line with His principles as they are revealed in His Word. That is why it is so important to learn how to walk by faith. Even though you are a tither, even though you give, if you do not know how to protect your investment in the Kingdom of God, the devil will continue to steal your return.

I was not raised in a Christian home. I did not go to church when I was a youngster, and all I ever heard about church at home was negative and bad. I did not get saved until the year I married.

After I was saved, I had a desire to please God. I wanted to do anything I could to please Him, because I was so happy that He had saved and redeemed me. I really did not know what redemption was all about; but the Word said it, so I accepted it.

When I first heard about tithing, I wanted to tithe. We struggled for years financially and economically. We did the best we knew how to tithe. I had read in the tenth verse of Malachi 3 where God said, ''I will open the windows of heaven and pour you out a blessing where there is not enough room to receive it.'' So I gave my tithes and sat with my arms folded waiting for God to drop the windows-of-heaven blessings down from heaven. I waited and waited, but they never came.

While I was waiting, the bill collector kept knocking on the door. While I was waiting, they jacked up the car and took it away! Another time they came and took the television. A man came into the house, unplugged our TV, picked it up, took it downstairs, put it on the truck, and left. I stood on the porch and waved good-bye! They took the car, the TV, and all the credit cards! I have been there, so I know what I am talking about.

I was sitting there waiting but nothing ever happened, and I could not figure out why. What I did not know was that I was not exercising any faith, nor did I know how to protect my investment. I did not know how to claim the blessings. As soon as you give, God's blessings are released automatically. However, we have an enemy, Satan, who seeks to devour and steal that which belongs to us. He is waiting. As soon as the blessing comes, he steals it from us. If you do not know how to use your faith and protect it, he will steal it from you and there will be nothing God can do about it.

The moment you give your tithe, God releases the windows-of-heaven blessings. There is a reciprocity, a reciprocal. The moment *you* give, *God* gives. It comes immediately. However, there is a time element involved. God is in the spirit world and that spirit world is outside the realm of the physical. The blessing has to come from the spirit world into the physical world. It is your faith that makes the transfer.

In the meantime, Satan is sitting out there, between the two worlds ready to steal your blessing as it comes in. The only way you can keep his hands off is with your faith, by confessing the Word and saying, "In the Name of Jesus, I believe I receive the windows-of-heaven blessings." When you do that, he cannot touch it. But until you do, he can steal it and there will be nothing God can do about it. God is pouring it out and you are not getting it because the devil is sitting there in between, stealing it from you.

To help further illuminate what I am talking about, I will give you an illustration that the Holy Spirit gave me. You know that you cannot plant a seed Monday morning and get a harvest Monday night. It does not work that way. Seeds do not grow that fast, but the moment you plant good seed into good ground, the germination process begins. When the elements within the seed and the soil begin to interact, germination immediately begins.

But wait a minute—the seed is under the ground and you cannot see it. A few weeks later as you go out to water the place where you have planted the seed, you notice that the earth is cracked in that area. The next day when you go out, the crack is a little wider. The following day you see a little green blade coming up.

In a few days it gets bigger and bigger until finally you see a plant coming up out of the ground. But when you saw the green blade coming up *is not* when it started growing. That is just when you had the privilege of first seeing it. The plant was growing all the time right there under the ground, but that ground hindered your eyes from actually seeing it.

Now you see, if you had been like some people, relative to spiritual things such as your tithes and offerings, you would say, "Well, ain't that somethin'! I planted that seed seven days ago and I don't see nothin' yet. Guess I'll just go ahead and plow this ground up, pour some concrete, and make a patio out of it." If you do, you will end up missing your blessings.

The seed is growing all the time, but it is under the ground. Your physical eyes cannot penetrate the ground, but you keep watering it and waiting. You know that the germination process started instantly. You know that the seed will grow, and very soon you will see the results.

Think of the spirit realm where God is as the ground through which your physical eyes cannot penetrate. Think of the seed as your tithes and offerings planted in that heavenly soil. Think of the confession of your mouth—"I believe I receive the windows-of-heaven blessings; I believe I receive the good-measure, pressed-down, shaken-together, and running-over blessings; I claim in the Name of Jesus, the hundred-fold return, and I believe that I receive it according to Mark 11:24"—as the watering process. You have to keep watering the seed.

The moment you gave your tithe God sent the windows-of-heaven blessings, but they had to come from the spirit world into the physical world. So you keep on watering.

With your physical eyes you cannot see into the spirit world, just as you cannot see into the ground, but the process is working all the time. Have faith. Believe it is working.

Believe your blessings are coming and make preparation to receive them. Since God is going to pour you out a blessing, you should have your baskets ready to receive the blessings. You have to use your faith. If you do not, Satan will steal your blessings.

Remember the story about the parable of the sower? Jesus described a sower who went forth to sow. When some seed fell by the wayside, what happened? Instantly the fowls of the air swooped down and plucked it up.

The devil is waiting to steal the seed—whatever seed you sow. In that story Jesus was using the seed as the Word, but the seed can also be the seed that you plant out of the fruit of your labor—your tithes and offerings. You have to use your faith.

As I said before, I thought for a long time that the white man was my problem. I thought those "blue-eyed devils" were stealing from me to keep me poor. It went like that for a long time. I tithed and tithed, but without any results. Then it became so bad that I could not afford to tithe anymore. That is when I really messed up!

Once I found out how to operate in the provisions that God had made, I was able to get out from under that curse.

The Travelers Insurance Company has a red umbrella as their trademark. Whenever you see a picture of that red umbrella, you will see rain falling on and around the umbrella. However, it is dry under the umbrella. In essence, they are saying:

There are rains of automobile accidents and disasters—many things that might happen to jeopardize you, your family, and your financial future. Come underneath the umbrella of Travelers Protection. Then when the rains start falling, it will not rain on you because you will be protected by the umbrella.

That is like the curse falling all around us. You can get underneath the umbrella of God's Word. Now the rains are falling all the time—the rains of adversity, the rains of poverty, the rains of fear. The umbrella *does not stop* the rain from falling, but it does stop the rain from falling on *you*, so you do not get wet.

I began to hoist my umbrella by putting tithing into operation. I began to tithe and claim the return on my tithes.

When we first started tithing, it was difficult. When I say "first started," I mean in these latter days after I had found out what God's Word said and learned how to operate in faith. It was difficult to tithe, because I still "owed my soul to the company store." Everything I had coming in was already owed for the next 24 months! I was just a messenger boy, picking up the check at the job and taking it to the creditors. That went on for days.

We decided that we were going to believe God and operate in the principles of God's Word to get out from under the curse. The job that I worked on at that time (just like most of you) took out payroll deductions.

They took out federal income tax and I never saw it. All I saw was a piece of paper with some figures on it.

As you very well know, the federal government (the IRS) allows you to take deductions for yourself, your wife, and your children. At that time there were five of us, including myself. So one year I decided to go without claiming *any* exemptions. We were already struggling, so it did not make much difference.

We learned to live on the little money that was left over. We let Uncle Sam save our money, because *I* sure could not save any. I figured as long as I did not get it, I could not spend it. I let them take it out ahead of time—before my hot little hands ever touched it. At the end of the year I filled out my income tax form, claimed my five exemptions, and received money back in one lump sum.

We looked over our assortment of bills. One bill that we were paying out on a monthly basis was enough money to allow us to tithe. So we paid off that one bill and started tithing.

We were right back in the same position, with no additional money. But now instead of paying that bill, we were paying our tithes. We started tithing and making the confession, "We believe we receive the windows-of-heaven blessings."

It was a while before we saw any appreciable change. But, remember, it takes time for your faith to grow to the point where it starts receiving the fruit from your planting into the Kingdom of God through tithes and offerings. There is a growth period in the spiritual realm, just as there is in the natural realm.

Let us say you want to produce apples. You plant an apple seed. It is going to take time in the natural for that tree to grow from a seed to the size where it is ready to produce fruit. You cannot plant it Monday morning and get fruit Tuesday afternoon. It does not work like that. You have to leave it there and let it grow.

Now, spiritual things are like that. It will take some time for the seed to develop into a fruit-bearing tree. But you know what? Once that tree reaches maturity and is ready to produce fruit, you will have a crop seasonally. You do not have to wait for it to grow up anymore, just go out with your baskets and pick the fruit. Then by pruning it, fertilizing it, weeding and trimming it, you can make it produce even more fruit.

Once the tree starts producing, you can look for a harvest all the time. Every year you can go out when the season is right and pick fruit to your heart's content. That is the way it works with the spiritual.

Maybe you do not want to wait for the growth—you want it right now. Do not misunderstand me—I know *why* you want it right now. When you first came into the knowledge of God's Word, you were already embroiled in problems and financial difficulties. You are under the pressure *now*, and you need to be bailed out *now*! But you know what? It will be well worth your while to take whatever steps are necessary to get into position to start operating in God's financial plan. It is *well* worth it.

We started doing that because we were determined to get out from under that curse. I found out that I was redeemed from the curse of the Law. When we rob God, we operate in the curse. Adam let the curse into the earth realm, but God has an umbrella that is well able to keep the curse off of us if we get under it.

When I pay my tithes, I put up that umbrella and the curse cannot touch me. It is not *God* cursing me, because I do not tithe. It is simply that the curse is already out there; and when I *do not* tithe, it is like being out from under the umbrella. If I get under the umbrella, I am where God can protect me.

You have to get under God's umbrella before God's power goes to work for you. Do not get mad and blame God for your problems. Get in line with His Word, then it will work for you.

So we began to tithe and operate in God's financial plan. I will be honest with you—it was a couple of years before we really saw any appreciable change. But think about this: If we had not tithed and started on God's financial plan, we would *never* have come out from under that curse. We could not be any worse off than we already were. Conditions were already in a deteriorating state and getting worse all the time. The only thing we had to lose was our present poverty condition.

Perhaps you are like we were, down and unable to go down any further. The only way you can go is up. We began to sow seed, and now we have a whole orchard full of trees bearing fruit! Every time I turn around, more fruit is coming in. Today we are above the situations. We are being blessed going out and coming in. We are free, and are going to be freer.

The windows-of-heaven blessings are coming in, and now we can be a blessing. I found out that it works. You can get into a position of being financially independent of the circumstances without having to hoodwink or con anybody, and you do not have to be ashamed of it. You can be right out in the open and aboveboard.

By following the principles that I have been sharing with you, I am in an excellent position. My every need is met, and I am able to give away more than 25% of every dollar I receive. Let me tell you—*that is fun!* Joy unspeakable and full of glory!

How did we get into that position? By observing what I am teaching you. By doing it. By taking the time to feed on God's Word. By putting into operation everything that I am telling you.

I was determined that if the windows-of-heaven blessings were true, I was going to benefit from them. I am here to tell you that it works. I am here to tell you that you must tithe. You cannot afford *not* to! In these closing days of time the economic squeeze is on. You had better learn how to operate in God's financial plan and stop robbing Him. I am so glad I stopped robbing God!

As I close this chapter, I want to share one thought from Proverbs 3:9:

> **Honour the LORD with thy substance, and with the firstfruits of *all* thine increase.**

Some of thine increase? No! *All* of it!

"Well, Brother Price, do you mean to tell me that if somebody gives me some money for my birthday that I have to tithe out of that?"

Far be it from me to say that you *have* to tithe out of it. You do not *have* to tithe anything. You can go on robbing God if you want to and live under that curse, but I think you are kind of stupid if you do.

I tithe out of everything I get. The first thing I think about when I see money is 25%, the part that goes to God. That is the first thing to enter my mind. If I find a dollar on the sidewalk, 25¢ belongs to God.

I do not tithe out of bondage, but out of love, appreciation, and obedience. I do it because *I want to!* Besides that, I like the results.

Honour the LORD with thy substance, and with the firstfruits of all thine increase.

Not the last fruits, not what is left over when you get through doing what you want to do. You are to honor the Lord with the firstfruits. If you honor God, He will honor you. Honor God with the firstfruits. That means whatever you get, the first part of it—before you spend any of it—ought to go to God.

"Will a man rob God?"

Have *you*?

Do you?

7
Where Is the Storehouse?

Malachi 3:10

Bring ye all the tithes into the storehouse, that there may be meat in mine house, and prove me now herewith, saith the LORD of hosts, if I will not open you the windows of heaven, and pour you out a blessing, that there shall not be room enough to receive it.

The Bible, whether you are aware of it or not, does not cover every contingency of life in a detailed manner.

What do I mean by that?

The Bible by virtue of its limitation in size could not cover every possibility of life. You ought to know that there are many things the Bible does not tell you to do. For instance, the Bible does not tell you to use deodorant. But it does give you some principles that you can apply to any situation in life.

Even with tithes and offerings, we do not have an abundance of detailed information about them. However, we do have *some* information. Many times the best way to operate is to go from the known to the unknown. You may not know what a certain thing means, or how to perform or function in it; but if you go from what you do know, you can move towards what you do not know.

To understand the meaning of "the storehouse" and where it is in our dispensation—the New Covenant day—we should be able to go back and find out what it meant in the day in which it was instituted.

Again, we look at the 10th verse of Malachi, chapter 3:

Bring ye all the tithes into the storehouse....

Notice two words, *all* and *storehouse*. Notice that the word *storehouse* is in the singular, indicating one. The word *all* means all of the tithes; it does not mean a part of the tithes, or a half of the tithes, or even a third of the tithes. *All* means all, because that is what *all* means. And God said bring them into the *storehouse*, singular. Apparently, that means there was only one storehouse at that time.

In researching this, I wanted to find out about this storehouse, because I had to make a relationship between what we know and do not know, in terms of the lack of detailed information given to us under the New Covenant.

The storehouse was located in the temple. There was only one temple at a time where God placed His name, though there were several temples built over a period of history. In that temple there were priests who ministered on behalf of the people.

Also in the temple was a place called "the treasury." The treasury was the storehouse, where the goods were placed, and there was only one of them. The goods were brought and placed on deposit there to be doled out to the people as they were needed.

As Christians we do not live under a system with a temple, like Israel. In fact, we collectively are called "a holy people, a holy nation, a peculiar people." We are the Body of Christ. Then individually, the Bible says, our bodies are the temples of the Holy Spirit. However, under the New Covenant we do have the local church, or local assemblies, places where the people gather together.

We have been instructed in the Bible to *forsake not* the assembling of ourselves together as some do. Under the New Covenant, we as individual Christians, based on our geographical location, have what we call church houses or church buildings, where we meet corporately. Why? To hear the Word of God, to praise the Lord, to sing praises unto God, to experience the gifts of the Spirit, to receive healing for our bodies if needed. We experience these things in the context of the local congregation.

Our local assembly for instance—the building we call Crenshaw Christian Center—is not the Church; the people are the Church. We just meet in the building. We have set the building apart, or sanctified it, to be a place of worship. We do not use it for a bowling alley, but for the worship of Almighty God. The building itself is not holy. It is only holy by virtue of the fact that *we* are in it. We make it holy by using it; otherwise it is just a building.

Each of the buildings called "the church" in a geographical location is the place where a particular group congregates together. After all, stop and think about it, the Church of Jesus Christ today is bigger than Israel was. There are more Christians in the world today than the number of Israelites at that time; and the geographical area then was relatively small when compared to Christians scattered all over the world today. It was not that difficult for them to make a pilgrimage to the temple once a year on the great Day of Atonement. But today we have the local church.

Now, why am I pointing out all of this? Because I received a letter one time which is very important to our subject. This letter reflects the thinking of many people. I include it in this chapter to draw an analogy from it. I want to use it as a point of clarification, because I am sure others (maybe even you) have thought along these same lines.

Taking into account what I have said about the storehouse, the treasury, the temple, the geographical location, the local congregations, the church houses that we meet in to minister and hear God's Word, I share this letter:

> Dear Pastor Price:
>
> Thanks be to God for you and the ministry of Crenshaw Christian Center.
>
> As you were teaching on tithes and offerings in the Sunday morning service, you said that God wants us to bring all the tithes into the storehouse, and not the storehouses. It confused me, so I asked God to make me understand what He was saying; James 1:7. I have been guilty of splitting up my tithes and offerings sometimes to support other ministers as the Holy Spirit leads. And this is what He said:
>
> "It is true there is only one storehouse as there is only one Body. Would you say that Kenneth Hagin, Rhema; World Evangelism; Jim Bakker, PTL Club; Pat Robertson, 700 Club; and Jimmy Swaggart are different bodies of Christ? No, there is only one Body, and only one storehouse. As the one Body of Christ is

geographically located in different places, so the one storehouse is geographically located in different places.''

As I bring and/or send my tithes and offerings as the Holy Spirit directs, they are going into the storehouse. As the early Church preached the same message with power, and in so doing won almost all the known civilized world in their day for Jesus Christ, so the latter Church will all have the same message with no schism to win this world for Jesus Christ.

Brother Price, I thank you for reading this letter as this was given to me by the Holy Spirit. Freely it was given to me, and freely I give it to you to use as you will.

It is a common practice among Christians to take their tithes and split them up. Each person is privileged to think and believe whatever they want, but based upon what I said about the temple, the treasury, the storehouse, and the local church, I cannot see that it would be right to take my tithe and split it up. Fred Price is not the storehouse. I am not the Body of Christ; I am a part of it. I am a member in particular of the Body of Christ, but I am not a storehouse unless your total spiritual sustenance is received from my ministry.

If you did not have a church or local congregation to go to—no church in your area that preaches the Word—that would be a different situation. Suppose your total spiritual feeding comes from our TV program or my books and tapes, then it would be okay to send your tithes to me or to my ministry if you wanted to and you would still get blessed for that, because this church would be your storehouse in that sense.

However, if you are a member of a local church and are adequately fed there, your primary obligation is to that local church. (I am not saying you do not receive benefit from other ministries such as apostles, prophets, evangelists and teachers.)

I personally do not believe that it is consistent with the Word of God to take the tithes you should be placing in your local church—your *primary* place of receiving—and split it up to give to some other ministry.

Do not misunderstand. I am not opposed to giving to other ministries—I do it myself—but I do not give my tithes. My tithes go to my local church; I give offerings to other ministries.

We have read in Malachi 3:10, "Bring ye *all* the tithes...."

All of it. If you make $100, your tithe would be $10. You put $2 in Crenshaw Christian Center, $1 in W's ministry, $3 in X's ministry, $3 in Y's ministry, and $1 in Z's ministry. You have used up your tithe, right? That is *not* bringing *all* the tithes. The verse said, "all the tithes," not a part of it.

If you split your tithes among various ministries that would not fulfill the injunction, "Bring ye *all* the tithes," because all of it would not be brought into *the storehouse*; it would be put into several *storehouses*. Individual men are not the Church; they are only a part of the Church. The local congregation where you receive your primary source of feeding is the place where your tithes should go.

I have gained from X's ministry. I get revelation from Y's ministry and others. I give to those ministries, and I support them. I believe in them, but I do not put my tithes into them. I put my tithes into Crenshaw Christian Center, because that is where I get my main feeding. I get fed every week. Every time I preach, I am feeding me. That is my church home, so I put my tithes there. I put offerings in other places.

I do not think that the letter we read would be consistent with what the Word says concerning the storehouse, the treasury, and bringing all the tithes. I am not locked into this, so I would not argue about it. You can do whatever you want. If you have a good conscience about it, if you can split up your tithes among five or six different ministries, wonderful—I cannot. Different strokes for different folks!

I do believe, however, that the Scripture warrants putting it all in one place, relative to the tithe. I think the word *all* qualifies it. "Bring ye *all* the tithes into the storehouse." Not *a* storehouse, but *the* storehouse. If I put it into *a* storehouse, my ministry might be one storehouse, X's ministry another storehouse, Y's ministry another, and so on. But then that would be "storehouses," wouldn't it? They are not the total, and neither am I. I am just a part of the Body of Christ, so if you put it into me, I would be only part of the storehouse.

As I said, if you have no storehouse—if there is no place where you live that gives you the Word—and you are feeding solely off of X's materials and are being blessed and instructed, then put your tithes there. Support the ministry that is supporting you with the Word of God. But when you find a storehouse—a local congregation where you can be a member and be adequately fed—your tithe should go to support that storehouse, so it can continue to preach the Word to others like you. You can always take offerings and put them other places.

I used the letter just to show another point of view, because I know from experience that people break up their tithes, and I do not believe it is right. However, you will have to be the final judge, based on what knowledge we *do* have in the Bible. Let us look again at Malachi 3, verses 8,9:

> **Will a man rob God? Yet ye have robbed me. But ye say, Wherein have we robbed thee? (God says) In tithes and offerings.**

> **Ye are cursed with a curse: for ye have robbed me, even this whole nation.**

Again, I point out that if you are not tithing, you are robbing God. That is a Bible fact. It is not Fred Price or Crenshaw Christian Center saying it. That is what the Bible says. Will a man rob God?

I did not write the book of Malachi. My name does not appear. *God* said, ''Will a man rob God?'' God is asking the question through the mouth of the Prophet. It is not even the Prophet saying it. God Almighty is speaking to His people through the mouth of His Prophet. He said:

> **Will a man rob God? Yet ye have robbed me. But ye say, Wherein have we robbed thee? (And God says) In tithes and offerings.**

That would say to me, if I am not tithing and if I am not giving offerings, I am robbing God. Notice that tithes come first. It says, ''tithes and offerings,'' not ''offerings and tithes.'' Then it says, ''Bring ye all the tithes into the storehouse.'' He did not necessarily say, ''Bring all the *offerings*.'' We can, but primarily the tithe goes into the storehouse.

The reason I am bringing this up again and laboring the issue is because I know personally that many people have financial problems. With our economy soaring out of sight like it is, the prices of goods and services are escalating every day.

I keep bringing up the question, ''Will a man rob God?'' because of the ninth verse. You may be having financial problems, yet you love the Lord. You are born again, filled with the Spirit, and go to church regularly. You read your Bible, attend Bible class, and witness to others about Jesus. You do good things. Your motive is right, yet you are having financial problems. You are working, your spouse is working, you may even have an extra job; but still you can barely make it. There must be a reason. *Maybe* it is because you are robbing God, and because you *are*, notice the ninth verse:

Ye are cursed with a curse....

If you are not tithing, you are operating under that curse. Now understand, it is not God putting the curse on you. The curse entered the human race in the Garden of Eden when Adam sinned. Remember, God gave us His Word as an umbrella to protect us from the curse. The umbrella of God's Word does not stop the curse anymore than an umbrella stops rain. What it does is stop you from getting wet—the important thing! The Covenant of God keeps you from being under that curse.

The curse is all around you, functioning and operating all the time, but it does not have to get on you if you take refuge under God's Covenant. It might be that your financial problem is because of that curse, and you may not even realize it, but it is still going to work against you.

There may be a can of gasoline on the ground. If you, thinking there is milk in the can, strike a match to look inside, you will find out quickly that it is gasoline! It does not matter whether you know it is gasoline or not. It is still going to explode, because that is the nature of gasoline fumes. When they are ignited, they explode.

Do you understand what I am saying? You may not realize that you are operating in the curse financially, but it will still strap you and keep you bogged down in a financial quagmire.

God wants you to be free, and the way to get free is through tithes and offerings. It is worth whatever it costs you to get into God's financial plan. It is worth going barefooted if necessary to get yourself into position to start tithing according to the Word of God. You cannot lose if you operate in God's financial plan. So, examine yourself and find out: Are *you* robbing God?

We looked at this before, but I want to stress it again. Proverbs, chapter 3, verse 9, says:

Honour the LORD with thy substance....

Did you know it is an honor to tithe? Now your motives have to be right. If your motive is to get rich quick, it will not work. Faith cannot operate through a wrong motive. You have to do it out of a desire to be obedient to the Word of God. You do it because you love God and appreciate what He has done for you.

Tithing is an area you have control over. You control what comes out of your pocket. You reach into your wallet. You write the checks.

You honor the Lord with your substance. Substance is that which is tangible, that which is material.

Honour the LORD with thy substance, and with the firstfruits of all thine increase.

This is not talking about spiritual things, but about substance. You honor the Lord with your firstfruits. That is the tithe. The tithe ought to come off the top. Some Christians make a mistake by trying to figure their tithes *after* they have paid everybody else. If you do that, I will guarantee, there will not be much left to pay the tithe. You have to learn that the tithe is first.

Now I realize that because you have not known how to operate this way in the past, you may be in bad financial straits. You may be like I was, unable to tithe without cutting somebody off or not paying your bills.

My friend, do not make that mistake. Remember tithing is not for God's benefit, it is primarily for yours. So do not fail to pay your bills. If you have made a contract to pay someone a certain amount of money on the 15th of each month, then pay it. You must honor your obligations. The worst testimony in the world is a Christian who will not pay his bills. You made a *promise.* You have that person's car, or his clothes, or his goods. You are already using them. You said you were going to pay him, so you should pay him. Do not stop paying him to start tithing. *That is not the way to do it!*

By the same token, stop adding to that account. Pay the thing off, then you will be in a position to tithe! Stop using the account. If at all possible, do without it for a while. We did. We made a quality decision to do without some things, in order to reach a goal, in order to get to the point where we could tithe.

When you start letting your tithe be first, then you will be in a position to operate in the fullness of God's provisions for your life.

It is like buying a home. How many times have you received your paycheck, then sat down and figured out *everything* you had to pay, waiting until the very last to figure out how you were going to pay your house payment? Not once! You probably work everything else around that house payment, because it is usually the biggest payment the average person has to pay.

You pay your house note first, because you know they will foreclose and put you in the street without thinking a thing about it. Houses are up for foreclosure every day. Houses are being sold for taxes because people cannot pay. It is simple: Pay it by a certain day, or they will take it and sell it to somebody else for the taxes owed on it.

You need to learn how to let your tithes be first, because you owe that to God. You are supposed to pay it just like you pay your house payment. **Learn to pay the tithe first.**

To me the tithe is first, and everything else revolves around it. The only money I have to spend is the amount left over after I pay my tithes. Whenever I get some money, the first thing I think of is the tithe.

You have to get into that position too, and you may have to *do* something to get to that place. If you were like I was when you first heard about tithing, you were already inundated with debt and had very little left over to pay tithes or even give an offering. Like I say, it may mean you have to do without some things so that you can pay off some bills before being able to tithe.

Start learning how to cast your bread upon the waters according to Ecclesiastes 11:1. Then, as it says, "...thou shalt find it after many days." Start casting it out. *At first* you might not see any results, but just keep on casting with your heart right as you exercise your faith. After a while you will look out and see that every wave coming in has a loaf of bread on it! Then you will rise above your financial circumstances. You will not have any more financial problems. You will be a recipient, and then a repository for the blessings of God as you start giving it away.

Honour the LORD with thy substance, and with the firstfruits of all thine increase.

Not the last, not just something left over after you have done what you want to do, but the *first*fruits. Then it says:

So shall thy barns be filled with plenty, and thy presses shall burst out with new wine.

You will have an abundant supply. Think about this: All God is asking for is a tithe, or a payment of

10%. Guess what? You get to keep 90%! That is a pretty good deal.

For several years interest rates have been higher than 10%. The prime interest rate—interest on home loans and other loans—has continually escalated over the years. It has gone up, up, up, up—and it will keep going up.

Think about the deal that God gives you. Recorded Biblical history, according to *Bishops Ushers Chronology**, going back to the Garden of Eden covers approximately 6,000 years. Just think that in 6,000 years God has never changed His interest rate. It has stayed at 10% for 6,000 years! What a deal! Only 10%. He never changed it. He never asked you for 10¼% or 11%. It has been 10% for 6,000 years.

That is a fabulous deal—only 10%, and you get to keep 90%! With your 90% you can give to all the ministries you want, but the tithe belongs to the Lord. It goes into the storehouse. The thing that is so grand and glorious about it is we even get benefit out of the 10%. You do not walk up to God and place that 10% in His big universal hand. No! You put it into the local church, into the storehouse.

Do you know what the tithe is for? To provide for the storehouse and keep it functioning, and to provide *you* with a comfortable place in which to receive the Word of God.

---

*James Usher from *Encyclopedia of Religion*, ed. Vergilius Fern (New York: The Philosophical Library, Inc., 1945), p. 807.

So you are still getting benefit out of the 10%. In fact, you are still getting benefit out of the 100%. Then on top of that, when you give God the 10%, He gives you an interest return—the windows-of-heaven blessings. You get the benefit going and coming. That is fabulous! You cannot lose. You cannot get a deal like that anywhere in the world, but Almighty God gives it to you.

God wants you to be blessed. It could be that because you are robbing God, you are operating under the curse and not getting the blessings of God.

So what is the tithe for? The tithe is for the support of the local church, and to bless you. Those are the two main purposes: to provide what is necessary to get the Gospel preached to the ends of the earth, and then to provide your needs. God wants your needs met and your desires, which are consistent with a godly life.

8
20%, The Penalty for Robbing God

We ended Chapter 7 by discussing where we should put the tithe. Where is the storehouse? I think we have made it dramatically clear that under the New Covenant dispensation the storehouse is the local church or sheepfold—the place where the congregation congregates, where they meet together, where the Word of God goes forth from the overseers whom God has set over the churches. The pastors are supposed to feed the sheep and the lambs.

The tithe should go to the storehouse. That way the storehouse can be maintained, and there will be meat in God's house—the meat of the Word. When people come into the storehouse, their hunger and thirst after righteousness will be satisfied, because the Word of God will be going forth under the anointing and quickening power of the Holy Spirit.

You and I have an obligation to survey carefully the storehouses, or supposed storehouses, and find out if they qualify as a place of deposit for our tithe which belongs to God. *Remember,* the tithe is not yours; it belongs to God. You are not the owner of the tithe, the 10%. You are the owner of the balance, because the 90% belongs to you.

You are encouraged to give an offering, and you can give your offering wherever you please, but you are told specifically to bring the tithes into the store-house. You will have to make a decision as to where the storehouse is. Unfortunately, every church or church house is not a storehouse. It is sad, but true, that in most churches you will receive nothing of the Word of God—no real guidance or instruction, no real information about how to live the overcoming and victorious Christian life, no understanding of the truth that makes one free.

You have to decide where the storehouse is, then make a decision to place your money there. That money (the tithe) belongs to the Lord, and you will give an account to Him for what you do with it. You are a steward of that 10%, of that tithe. You have been entrusted with it, and you will give an account of your stewardship.

You have to decide where the storehouse is. You have to make a value judgment and decide, "Does this place qualify as the storehouse?" *If it does not,* you had better be careful about where you are putting God's money. I see people put their money into things that are far from being the storehouse.

The storehouse should be a place where people can continually go and be fed spiritually. As a result, spiritual births will be taking place constantly—new life will be coming forth. The sheep will be fed; and when the sheep are fed, they will give birth to lambs. There will constantly be a new crop coming in.

You see, many people are conditioned to going to church out of tradition, out of custom. God forbid that they should miss church on Sunday morning, even though they are not receiving a thing. They are just going out of conscience. They go in spiritually hungry and come out spiritually starved. It is sad.

But we have to make a decision as to where we put the Lord's money. God clearly tells us in His Word that we should not give the tithe just anywhere. We need to make a value judgment as to whether this place, wherever it is, qualifies as a house of God—as a sheepfold, as a storehouse.

Some Christians have been tithing to certain denominations all their lives. They think, "Mama was one. Grandpa was one. I was raised one." Some have even said, "I was born one and I will die one." That is fine as long as *that* one is the right one. Be sure that you are putting God's money where it belongs.

At the outset of this book, we referred to Deuteronomy, chapter 26. In that chapter it talks about the tithe and the offering. It talks about what the people were supposed to do when they entered into the land that the Lord was going to give them and how they were to bring their offerings to the house where God had placed His Name. They were to bring their tithes to the high priest of those days and make a profession with their mouths. The priest was supposed to take it, put it in a basket, go before the heavenly Father, and worship Him with it.

Throughout the 26th chapter of Deuteronomy, it talks about that. But there is one statement that is absolutely astounding in its import. We need to examine it very carefully.

143

Deuteronomy 26:14

I have not eaten thereof in my mourning, neither have I taken away aught thereof for any unclean use, nor given aught thereof for the dead: But I have hearkened to the voice of the LORD my God, and have done according to all that thou hast commanded me.

When you read the context, you will find that it is talking about the tithe. Now we will read this verse from *The Amplified Bible,** which brings a clarity to it that is most revealing.

Deuteronomy 26:14 (AMP)

"I have not eaten of the tithe in my mourning [making the tithe unclean], nor have I handled any of it when I was unclean, or given any of it to the dead...."

Unfortunately, there are many churches which are D-E-A-DOUBLE D...DEAD! There is no life and no anointing in them. As a consequence, to put money there would be giving it to the dead; and the Bible says do not give it to the dead. If it were alive, it would be producing life.

Many churches are dead, and you cannot afford to put God's money in them. To do that is like taking your money and flushing it down the toilet. It is the same thing. You have been putting your money in a dead place, in a mausoleum, in a graveyard. God said not to do that, not with *His* money.

Now look at Deuteronomy 26:14 again:

I have not eaten thereof in my mourning....

The Amplified Bible, Old Testament (Grand Rapids: Zondervan, 1962, 1964), p. 244.

In other words, when the pressure was on—when life seemed to be inundating them, when circumstances were so heavy upon them and it seemed like they were going down—it was like being in a state of mourning. They said, "...I have not eaten thereof...." In other words, they did not take the tithe and eat it up during that period of time while they were in mourning. They said further:

> ...neither have I taken away aught thereof for any unclean use....

In other words, they said, "I have not taken any part of the tithe and put it into an unclean use." Then they said:

> ...nor given aught thereof (any of it) for the dead....

In other words, it was saying, "Don't give into a dead church where there is no life."

"But, Brother Price, you do not understand. Grandma was one and Great-Granddaddy was one. I was raised in that church. I have always gone to church there. After all, this church has been established for the last 37 years."

Listen to me, friend. God is not impressed with your church's longevity. He is not impressed with the name over your church door. That does not move God. There are graveyards that have been in business a long time too, but they are still graveyards.

When you put God's money into a place, you have to consider where you are putting it. You are responsible for it, and God is going to hold you accountable for it.

God said do not give it to the dead, so you have to make a decision: "This ministry, this church that I am supporting—is it dead or alive? Is it producing?" *You* have to make that decision, because *you* are the one responsible for it.

If you make a hundred dollars, then 10% belongs to the Lord and 90% is left to you. If you want to give *your* money to the dead, that is your business. You have the privilege to do that, because it is *your* money. Based on your will, you *can* give it to the dead. But, my friend, the tithe belongs to the Lord. It should be going into a storehouse—a place where the meat is stored, where people can gain knowledge and understanding about the things of God, where something is happening, where life is, where the anointing of the Spirit of God is.

It is easy to determine if a place is really a storehouse. It does not take long. Just listen for a few moments to what is being said. Listen to the songs that are being sung. Listen to the preacher. Listen to the announcements. You can soon tell whether or not the Holy Spirit has first place there. If you *cannot* tell, you are in serious trouble and need to check *yourself* out.

I have listened to much Christian radio and TV. It does not take long to ascertain where a person is coming from. Understand this: we are not dealing with the sincerity of any persons involved. We are not talking about whether or not they are saved, or whether or not they are going to heaven. We are not talking about the fact that their names are written in the Lamb's Book of Life. We are not talking about whether or not they love the Lord. That is not even being brought into question. We dare not judge that. I do not know what is in their hearts, so I give them the benefit of the doubt.

But I know that you can love the Lord and be just as wrong as a three-dollar bill in terms of how you are operating in the Kingdom of God. I was one of them. I would defy anybody to tell me I did not love the Lord, but I was not walking in line with His Word. I was walking in line with tradition. I was going by what the saints told me and sometimes ''the saints ain't.''

If a church is alive, if the Word of God has free course and the Holy Spirit is allowed to take His rightful place in the midst of the congregation, there will be some fruit resulting from it. After all, Jesus said a tree is known by its fruit. If after 45 years there is nothing on the limbs, it must be a dead tree—something is wrong. How many years does it take to find out that a tree is not producing any apples?

Jesus told a parable about a man who went out to the orchard and said to the man taking care of his fruit trees, ''I have come to this tree for three years in a row and there is no fruit on it. Cut it down.'' The vinedresser said, ''Master, give it one more year. Let me weed it, fertilize it, water it, prune it, trim it back one more year. If after a year, it produces no fruit, I will cut it down.''

Do you know what happens when a church does not follow the Word of God and does not operate in line with God's prescribed program? Every church has a candlestick, a lamp stand; and every church has an angel. God calls that angel back and removes the lamp stand. Do you know why He does it? So that it will die and get out of the way. Then the road will be uncluttered for those who are coming through doing it God's way.

Look around. You will see many of them, and they are barely holding on. Some have been holding on for 25 years. Again, we are not dealing with the sincerity of the people involved; but, friend, if you are not doing it God's way, it will not work. You have a decision to make: Where will you put *God's* tithe?

Maybe you heard about tithing many years ago like I did. I was in a church that really did not teach anything about tithing. They just said we ought to tithe and read the scripture, "Will a man rob God?" That shook me up because I had robbed other people of some things that belonged to them and the police had put me in jail swiftly. So I did not want to mess up with God and be put in His jail, wherever that was. I did not like the one downtown, and I sure did not want to go to God's jail!

So, almost out of fear, I began to tithe. Of course, I desired to follow the will of God. I wanted to do what was right. Not knowing what to do, I believed anything the preacher told me. He read it in the Bible, but he never really instructed us in it. I knew nothing about claiming the windows-of-heaven blessings. I did not know that a curse would result if I did not follow the Word of God.

As I said before, the curse is out there and I have no immunity from it if I am not walking in line with God's Word. If I am walking in line with God's Word, it is like taking a shot that makes me immune to the disease germs that are going around.

I began to tithe, because I wanted to do it. I did not really know anything about *how* to do it. I just did it anyway. My finances were already in a mess, so when I started paying my tithes by giving 10% to the church, I barely had enough money left to pay the bills.

Do you know what finally happened? You may have experienced this too. Eventually, I reached the point where I could not afford to tithe anymore. So I stopped. I said, "There ain't no point in me giving God ten dollars—I only make a hundred! I will give Him a dollar and use the nine to pay some bills." That seemed reasonable to me. After all, God did not need the money.

Unfortunately, I did not realize that tithing and offerings are not for God's benefit, but for *ours*. He does not need it, but it is through our giving it that He has a channel through which to bless us in the areas of material things.

I stopped tithing, and it went like that for a long time. Without knowing it, I was not only robbing God, but myself also. I was in a financial situation from which I could not extricate myself; and I did not understand why things were not working for me, financially and materially. Every deal that I made would fall through. I was doing everything I knew to do. It was a hard way to go, and I could not figure out what was wrong.

God in His infinite wisdom knew we would be tempted into not paying our tithes, even after we knew that we should, so He built a penalty clause into the contract. Many people do not know that.

Not only was I robbing God, but I compounded the robbery by operating in the penalty for the robbery. So I was getting it on two counts. The federal government had me and also the state.

Sometimes when a crime is committed, it is under both federal and state jurisdiction at the same time. When the state gets through throwing the book at you, then the federal government takes over. They could add another 99 years to your sentence. You are wiped out both ways.

That is how it was with me spiritually. I was not only robbing God and operating under that curse, but I was compounding the robbery by operating in the penalty.

Every financial program has a penalty clause attached to it, even if you are buying a home. For instance, you may have a thirty-year mortgage on your house with an ordinary standard fixed rate of interest. If you pay that house off before thirty years, there is a penalty involved. It is called a prepayment penalty. People make their money on the interest. If you pay off the house too quickly, they will not make as much money on the interest as they would if you kept the mortgage for thirty years. So they make you pay this prepayment penalty for paying it off ahead of time.

Every financial program has a penalty. If you have a treasury bill account, or T-bill account, then you have to leave your money in it for six months. Take it out before six months, and you will incur a penalty.

God has a penalty, and if you are not operating in line with His Word, then you come under that penalty clause. Now I want to show you the penalty.

Let me say this: Sometimes if you do not understand, you might think, "My goodness, all that preacher is doing is preaching those folks into conviction, putting them under bondage and trying to put them in a bag." No, I am trying to get you *out* of the bag. I am trying to get you to a point where you can operate in the freedom that God has provided for you.

Listen, friend, you had better get yourself together. Things are getting worse by the day economically. If you do not learn how to operate in God's financial plan, you are going to be left with the short end of a big fat stick. You had better learn because these economic times are getting worse, and you will have to learn how to supernaturally believe for the things that you need.

That is why I am mentioning about this. I am not trying to put you in bondage. I am not trying to make you feel guilty. I am not bringing these things up so you will drag your tail between your legs, crawling on your hands and knees and feeling bad about it. I am trying to show you how you can get out of the financial quagmire you are in and stop robbing God.

Maybe you did not know about the curse, but that is no excuse—you are still going to operate in it. I am trying to show you how you can get out and rise above it.

If you are charged $2.50 a gallon for gasoline, it will not make any difference to you, because your

Father will provide for you to have more than enough. That is what I am saying.

That is why I am talking about it. It is not my intent to make you feel guilty or put you in bondage, but to show you how to be free. I found out how to be free. I am free! Free at last—free at last! Thank God Almighty, I am free at last! Free in my spirit! Free in my soul! Free in my body! Free in my wallet!

How did I get there? By observing what I am telling you right now. That is why I am sharing it with you, so you can get in on it. I was robbing God. I did not know that I was robbing Him. It was not my intention to rob Him. But the curse was whipping me in every way and I did not know what it was. The churches I went to were not telling me anything about how to walk in the power of God. They did not tell me, so I did not know.

The devil had me whipped. He walked on me and spit on me until the day a man came along preaching the Word of God—the uncompromising Gospel of the Lord Jesus Christ—and showed me how to be free. I grabbed hold of that like a hungry dog would grab a bone. I started running with it and have run until I have shed all the shackles. Today I am as free as a bird! Hallelujah! Free, free, free!

That is why I am sharing it. I robbed God, then I compounded the robbery by operating in the penalty. I stopped tithing and started using the money. I said, "Well, after all, God does not need this money, so I will just give a dollar."

God knew there would be a great temptation on our part, simply because we are the trustees of His money. We have it in our hands. When you have it in your hand and are looking at your needs, at all the things you have to pay, it is a temptation to take God's money and use it for yourself. Of course, you always have the intention of paying it back. I can tell you from experience that paying back is the hardest game in the world to win. It is a hard game to catch up with.

The best thing to do is never get in the bag. It is so hard to pay back. "Well," you say, "if I could just borrow this." So, you borrow it, forgetting that you have to pay back the borrow, plus everything else. It gets worse and worse.

But God recognized that there would be a temptation on our part to take His money, to borrow from the tithe. So God built a penalty into it to discourage anybody from borrowing on His tithes. Let us read about it as found in Leviticus, the 27th chapter.

Leviticus 27:30,31

And all the tithe of the land, whether of the seed of the land, or of the fruit of the tree, is the LORD'S: it is holy unto the LORD.

And if a man will at all redeem aught of his tithes, he shall add thereto the fifth part (or 20%) thereof.

Verse 31 is very interesting. The implication is that a man has taken the tithe and used part of it for other things. If you did that in our society, you could be arrested for misappropriation of funds. That is what you would be doing with *God's money*.

I was a chief exponent of robbing God and then operating in this penalty. A number one example of a chump—that is what I was. I did not realize that I was robbing God. I figured I could get away with it, because God did not drop a hammer on me. I did not know that the hammer had been dropped all the time.

As soon as I had started doing that, the umbrella of God's protection had folded and I was operating in that curse without knowing it. I could not figure out why I was having such a hard time. It was because I was operating in that curse. I was cursed because I was robbing God.

Again, verse 31 says:

> **And if a man will at all redeem aught of his tithes, he shall add thereto** (to that which he redeems) **the fifth part thereof.**

That is 20%. So that means 10% plus 20%, or 30%. It is a lot better to give ten than to have to redeem it.

Well, I can tell you, I found out what was going on and I got my game together. Now I tithe 25% of all my income plus offerings. What did the verse say? A fifth? That is 20%! It is cheaper to pay the 10%. Like I said, I am not telling you this to put you in bondage or shame you or put you in a bag. I am trying to help you get out of whatever circumstances or situation you might be in.

Many of you know I am telling you the truth. You have been doing everything you could for the last several years. Though some of you are working on two jobs, you still cannot make ends meet. You are not really getting ahead; you are struggling. But you do not have to struggle. I am well persuaded that God does not intend for His kids to struggle. There is more than enough of this world's goods for you to have plenty.

Someone says, "That will work for you because you are a preacher." But that is foolishness.

A member of our church, just a lay person, came to me and told me how he and his wife got into the Word of faith and began to believe God's Word. Then a situation arose in their economics and they needed $1,200.

One day as he was working at his machine, a man walked up to him and said, "The Lord has spoken to me and told me to give you $1,200. How do you want it? Cash or check."

He said, "I will take it in pennies!"

Twelve hundred bucks! That man is not a preacher; he is just a lay person—but he is believing God!

I am sure there are many Christians who can testify how God has blessed them over and over and over again—and they are not preachers. They could get business when nobody else could. Businesses were going bankrupt while they had so much they could not take it all.

We Christians can have it when nobody else can. You ought to have it! You are a king's kid!

I trust that if you are in this situation, you do not get in bondage. This is not to put you in bondage. If you do not know anything about tithing—have never even heard of it—then start out *from now*. But, if you have known about tithing—have known that you should do it—then deliberately took God's money and spent it for yourself, you have no excuse. Just like me—I knew I was not doing what the Word said. I just took God's money and deliberately spent it on myself. When I say "myself," I was trying to pay some bills; but it was my fault. *I* made the bills. The bills did not make themselves.

Now, referring again to Leviticus 27:31, it says:

And if a man will at all redeem aught of his tithes, he shall add thereto the fifth part thereof.

Does this mean he shall add the fifth part to the original amount of money that the tithe was taken from, or to the total tithe, or what?

It is talking about redeeming the tithe itself, not the money that the tithe came from originally. Let us say I made $100. My tithe would be $10. Then let us say I decided to give $5 of the tithe and keep the other $5 to help pay a bill. If I took $5, that means I am short $5 in my tithes. I have to make it up. I have stolen from God, taking what belonged to Him. Remember, the tithe is the Lord's. I took the Lord's money and used it for another purpose.

If I want to stay in a position where my channels will continue to be open and God can bless me with the windows-of-heaven blessings, then I have to unclog that channel. I have to keep that channel free by making up the $5. That means I would have to pay back the $5 plus the fifth part, or 20%, of $5. How much would that be? One dollar. I would have to pay back $6.

Now consider the person who stole the whole tithe from the Lord. He did not give any of it. For instance, he made $100, so the tithe was $10. But he took it and used it all for his own purpose. So he owed $10 plus a fifth part, or 20%. That meant he owed the $10 tithe plus $2, or a total of $12.

You have to take the part of the tithe you did not give to God and add a fifth part to it. When you get to the point of giving large amounts of money, that 20% starts adding up. You will find that it is more reasonable to pay the tithe than it is to pay the penalty.

9
Deposits and Withdrawals

Jesus told us that we have a heavenly bank account and that we should lay up treasures in heaven.

There are two basic ways to make deposits into the heavenly bank account: tithes and offerings, or investing into the Gospel. The tithes go into the local storehouse, the offerings into the Gospel for the support of the ministry. It can go into the same storehouse where the tithe goes or into other ministries in other places.

Mark 10:28

Then Peter began to say unto him (Jesus), Lo, we have left all, and have followed thee.

Whether you realize it or not, the Apostle Peter was a businessman. He was in the fishing business with John and others on the Sea of Galilee. They made their livelihood by catching and selling fish.

Notice what Peter says to Jesus:

Lo, we have left all, and have followed thee.

In other words, he said, "We have left our business, our means of livelihood. We have left the opportunity to perhaps become rich men. We have left it all to follow You."

Verse 29

And Jesus answered and said, Verily I say unto you, There is no man that hath left house, or brethren, or sisters, or father, or mother, or wife, or children, or lands, for my sake, and the gospel's (sake).

This, of course, would have to include money, because money would be tied up in houses and lands. "Hath left" means that you have separated yourself from the house, the parents, the sisters, the wife, the mother, the lands and the money.

Verse 30

But he shall receive an hundredfold *now...*

Not 10%, but one hundredfold. When? N-O-W. He will receive a hundredfold—not after a while or by and by, not over there on the other side, not in heaven after you die, not when Jesus comes back and establishes the Kingdom, but *now*—present tense. Thank God! *Now in this time* (or in this life).

What is he going to receive a hundredfold of? Houses, brethren, sisters, mothers, children, and lands. But he shall receive them "with persecutions; and in the world to come eternal life."

But we can handle the persecutions. Persecutions are simply the pressure tactics Satan will try to put on us through the circumstances to try to discourage us and keep us from following the things of God and of Christ.

Those are the devil's tactics, but we can handle them—Jesus did. He showed us how to do it. He took authority over all the powers of darkness that tried to impede His progress. They never stopped Him from getting the job done. He went right on through and did what God called Him to do—and so can you!

Notice what Jesus said: We will receive a hundredfold now in this life. Not later, but now. You ought to know that if the Man said you would receive a hundredfold now—houses and lands and sisters and mothers and brothers—He must want you to have them, so it cannot be wrong to have them.

It would be wrong if your motive was wrong. If you just wanted to have them for the sake of having them and were not interested in *following Him*, then you would have a problem. But if you are following Him and are seeking first the Kingdom, the rest of the things should follow.

Jesus told us to expect a hundredfold return. That means a hundred times. Whatever it is, just multiply it by a hundred!

Luke 6:38
Give, and it shall be given unto you....

Stop right here. I want you to notice the enunciation of a spiritual law—the law of giving and receiving, the law of sowing and reaping. *Give, and it shall be given unto you....*

Turn that around and the opposite would be true. "*Do not* give, and it *will not* be given unto you."

Now there was a time when I was a penny-pinching tightwad. There was a time when I would not give a dime. In fact, I would not give anybody anything. Not even the time of day! Do you know why?

Because I never had anything. What little I did have came so hard and cost me so much.

I said, "Every dog for himself. Get it the best way you can. I am not giving you anything." That was my attitude, but I did not know that I was sealing my own doom with that attitude. You see, I had let greed rise up. I thought that the way to *get* things was by not giving anything, by simply keeping what you had. So *I would not give anything*.

My wife, on the other hand, has always been a giver. Though she did not know how to believe God for the return on her giving, she always had a spirit of giving. If I do not watch her, she will give everything away—all of it! Talk about a giving spirit! She has three of them! She will give everything away, me and the kids included!

But I would not give anything. Without knowing it, I was hanging myself. I did not know the secret, Luke 6:38. Again, it reads:

> Give, and it shall be given unto you; good measure, pressed down, and shaken together, and running over, shall men give into your bosom.

Now Jesus said, "Give, and it shall be given unto you," but He did not stop there. It would have been enough if He had said, "It shall be given unto you, period," but He went on to say, "It shall be given unto you *good measure*."

That too would have been enough, but He did not stop with "good measure." He said, "pressed down." Have you ever had to empty the trash, but when you opened the trash can to put in more, it was full, all the way to the top? You thought, "How am I going to get any more in there?" Then you got brave. You climbed over the edge of the trash can and started jumping up and down on the trash.

When you had finished packing it down, you discovered that the can was actually only half full. After you had squashed all the air pockets out, there was room to put more in. That is what God is saying to you. It will be given to you "good measure, *pressed down.*"

But He did not stop there. Then He said it would be "shaken together." That would compact it even more so. After that, He said it would be "running over."

Notice it says, "...running over *shall men give* into your bosom." Men will be the ones who give it to you. God will be speaking to those men, but the blessings will come through the hands of men.

Do not be like me. I used to think God would drop it out of the sky, but He never did. I believed the devil's lie when he said, "Well, the Lord did not want you to have it. He wanted to keep you humble, so He did not give it to you." I used to have that weird idea.

If you do not know what the Word says (and I did not!), it is easy to believe dumb things like that. The Word tells you how the blessings will come. Jesus said that men shall give into your bosom. It will come through the hands of a man, but it will be God speaking to the heart of that man, telling him to give it to you. It could be your employer giving you a bonus.

It could be somebody walking up and handing you some money.

I have experienced it many, many times. I really do not care what the man looks like who brings it. He can be black, white, brown, yellow, green, or polka-dotted! It does not make me any difference as long as he is a faithful channel. I receive because that is what Jesus said: men shall give into your bosom.

Now notice the rest of verse 38:

...For (or because) **with the same measure, that ye mete** (or measure out) **withal it shall be measured to you again.**

Remember, the incoming is based on the outgoing. If you do not like the incoming, you had better change the outgoing, because Jesus said, "...For with the same measure..."

Notice, it says, "with the *same* measure." Not one *like* it. Not one *similar* to it. Jesus said "with the *same* measure." If you have not been receiving anything, you can see why. It is because you have not been giving anything, you penny-pinching tightwad! You give God a dime, then think you have given Him too much.

Like I said before, that is how I used to be. I figured that God did not need the money like I did, so by holding on to it, I would get more. But I found out that when you hold on to it, you get nothing.

That is like standing in front of the fireplace, holding on to the firewood. You will not get any heat out of the fireplace until you put the wood into it and strike a match. You cannot stand in the middle of a room with wood in your hand and say to the fireplace, "Give me some heat and I will give you some wood!'' No! When you give wood to the fireplace, then the fireplace will give you some heat. That is the way it works.

Jesus said, ''Give, and it shall be given unto you; good measure, pressed down, and shaken together, and running over, shall men give into your bosom. For (or because) with the same measure that you measure it out it will be measured back to you again.''

When you start giving big, you will receive big. If you do not like the way you are receiving, or the amounts that are coming back, all you have to do is change what is going out.

Remember, *you* are the one who controls what is going out. If you do not like what is coming back, *you* are the one who will have to change what is going out. I believe in receiving big; so if I want to receive big, I have to give big. I give in large quantities, because I like to receive in large quantities. When I receive in large quantities, I have even more to give in large quantities. Then it becomes self-perpetuating.

Now remember, Jesus promised a hundredfold return. For whom? Those who give ''for My sake and the Gospel's.'' Everyone is not called to be in full-time ministerial service. Everyone is not going to be a pastor, or an apostle, or a missionary. The Bible tells us that: ''For God hath set *some* in the church.'' (Eph. 4:11.) Not all, but some. However, every Christian can preach. *Preach* means to verbally proclaim the Good News. Everyone who is born again can and should be doing that.

Even though you may not be one of those set in the Church to be a minister, you can be the support of a minister. Then for everything that minister accomplishes in the ministry, you will get credit for if you have been supporting it. Some people sit in church never taking into account that they are involved in every person who responds to the invitation given by the minister.

If you place your tithe in your local storehouse, give regularly to the support of that ministry, pray for it, and are involved with it in any way, you get credit for every person who responds to the invitation to come to Christ.

God calls one person to one job, and another person to another job. When we give into teaching and traveling ministries, we are helping them. By our financial support, we are going with them, because it takes finances to get them where they are going.

In Mark 16:15 Jesus says:

...Go ye into all the world, and preach the gospel to every creature.

I am glad He said *every* creature. He meant every white man CREATURE, every black man CREATURE, every red man CREATURE, every yellow man CREATURE, and every brown man CREATURE. If you were not made by General Motors, then you are a creature. If you are not a machine, then you are a creature. If you are species homosapien, then you are a creature and you have a right to have the Gospel preached to you.

Jesus said, "Go," and there is more than one way to go. We live in an age when we are even more blessed than the apostles were when Jesus spoke to them. The only way they could go was physically. Today we can send the Gospel around the world by satellite television, on cassette and reel-to-reel tape, on phonograph records, in books, in pamphlets and tracts. There are many ways available to us, and all of them cost money.

We can go by supporting the ministers who are called to go. As we minister to their physical and material needs, they are able to minister spiritual things to the people that they are sent to. Jesus said, "Go into all the world and preach the Gospel to every creature." When we give so that others can go, we go too and that is investing in the Gospel.

Romans 10:14,15

How then shall they call on him in whom they have not believed? and how shall they believe in him of whom they have not heard? and how shall they hear without a preacher?

And how shall they preach, except they be sent?

"...except they be *sent*." Now the "sending" can be done two ways: God sends by calling *you* to go, or you help send others by financing them to go where they are *called* to go. Can you see that?

Verse 15 again:

And how shall they preach, except they be sent? as it is written, How beautiful are the feet of them that preach the gospel of peace, and bring glad tidings of good things!

Verse 17

So then faith cometh by hearing, and hearing by the Word of God.

We support ministries knowing that when we give into ministries, we give for Jesus' sake and for the Gospel. That is the second way to make deposits into our heavenly bank account.

The tithe goes for the support of the local storehouse, so that the sheep coming there can continue to give birth to new lambs and new life can take place. But there are those who go out into other places and other areas, into virgin territory, that need to be supported.

Give, and it shall be given to you again. But how are you going to get it so you can have it to give? You may be like I was. I have sat in services and choked back the tears because I had nothing to give when an appeal was made. I sat there and maintained my composure, trying to look cool, but inside I was crying, because I could not give anything. We desired to give, but did not have it *yet*. We were confessing, we were believing, we could see it by faith, but we did not have it in manifestation.

Inside I would be crying, "Oh, I want to give." Not just because somebody else was giving, but because I wanted to be a part of it. I wanted to get involved, but I did not have enough to pay my bills, let alone give.

I said, "The day will come when I will be able to write out a check for $1,000 and just give it away. I will not just be a sponge, always soaking it up; but I will be able to give it out." I said by faith it would happen and, praise God, it has! I have written checks for $10,000 and given them away! And that is not the biggest one *I am going* to write. I am saying it now with my mouth because I believe it in my heart, the day will come when I will write one for $25,000 and give it into a ministry.

I believe in what I am telling you. I know it works, and you can get involved in it. It will take care of all your own needs, then you will have it to give away. That is when the fun begins! This is not something for *you* to get for *yourself* and sit in the corner with. The point is for you to get into a position where you can be a channel of blessing.

But how are you going to bless somebody else if you are not blessed yourself? How are you going to give it when you do not have it? You have to get to the point where you have it.

God has made a method available, and I am teaching it to you right now. Get involved with it! You say, "I cannot afford to tithe!" I am here to tell you, you cannot afford *not* to tithe. You cannot afford *not* to be a giver.

Now let me say this, if you owe bills for which you have already made contractual arrangements, pay those bills. I do not care how much you want to tithe. Do not take money that belongs to your car payment, or your house payment, or other payments and tithe with it. *That is not the way to do it!*

You say, "Well, I cannot tithe." You do not have to start out tithing if you are not able to do it. God knows you just found out about tithing and you are up to your neck in debt. He knows you cannot do it without letting your bills go. What a witness that would be! Here you come, Mr. Christian, with your "one way" symbol on your checks, and you do not pay your bills. That is not a very good testimony.

I will show you a simple formula on how to do it. One thing that hangs up many people is wanting to start out at the top. You do not start anything at the top. You start at the bottom and work your way up.

Now you may say: "Well, I want to tithe. I believe everything you say, Brother Price. I see it in the Bible, and my heart witnesses to it. But I cannot tithe. I am so strapped financially. I am having trouble paying my bills and I cannot afford to give 10%. If I give 10%, something is going to go unpaid. What can I do?"

Start getting out of debt!

"But that is going to take time!"

You are right.

"What can I do in the meantime about giving?"

I am glad you asked that question. I have the answer for you. Are you ready? Now what did Jesus say? He said if you leave, or give up, things "for My sake, and the Gospel's," you will receive a hundred-fold. Here is how you can start out. Do you have a nickel? Sure you do! You can find a nickel somewhere, and it will not take away from anything else.

This might sound comical, but I am not trying to be funny. I am trying to give you a practical way out of your financial dilemma. If you will take note of what

I am telling you and put it into operation, it will be just a matter of time until you are able to write out a check for $10,000 and give it away. When you can give it away, your own bills will already have been paid in full and you will still have money left in the bank.

Take 5¢, give it for Jesus' sake and the Gospel's, and claim your hundredfold return. Begin to believe God for the hundredfold return, and do not settle for anything short of it.

Now, how much is 5¢ times one hundred? $5. You now have $4.95 that you did not have before. $4.95 will not make that much difference on your bills, so treat it as though it were a separate item, independent of everything else you are doing.

Keep on struggling. Keep on making your payments the best you can. When you have the $5, take it and give it into the Gospel for Jesus' sake and claim your hundredfold return.

One hundred times $5 is how much? $500! Now you have $495.95 that you did not have when you began. Just keep on struggling with your bills and your daily routine; the 5¢ deal is a separate transaction.

The temptation at this point would be, of course, to take some of that $500 and apply it to some of those bills. Forget it! That time will come, but not yet. Take that $500, put it into a ministry, and claim the hundredfold return on it. Now one hundred times $500 is $50,000! That will even pay off *your* little Mickey Mouse bills.

Now you are rolling! You are ready to start whacking off those bills. Because everything is not going out of your paycheck, you can start tithing. *Now* you have the windows-of-heaven blessings coming down from above. You have the good-measure, pressed-down, shaken-together, and running-over blessings and the hundredfold return coming in. *How can you lose?*

That is how it works. That is exactly what I did. I did not have it to give, but I gave what I had. I started claiming it, confessing it, and by faith seeing it come in. I began to cast my bread upon the waters, knowing that after many days I would find it again. I kept doing that until it started coming back. That is how I got the $10,000 to give away.

I started this process some years ago, and I know it will work! That is why I am sharing it with you.

Now let me show you how to make withdrawals from your heavenly bank account, or how to receive from your giving. There are five things to remember, five things to employ in the financial plan of God, that will insure that you receive your heavenly withdrawals.

Number one: *Decide What You Need.*

The reason you may not be receiving anything is because you do not have your mind made up.

You do not go to the store and say to the grocer, ''Give me some of that!'' When he asks, ''How much do you want?'' you cannot just answer, ''I do not know, just give me some.'' You will not receive much of anything that way. You have to be specific about things.

You do not go into a restaurant, look at the menu, and say, ''Bring me some food!'' No! I say, ''I want some of that and some of that. Leave off that and add some of that." You have to be specific.

James 1:7,8

For let not that man think that he shall receive any thing of the Lord.

A double minded man is unstable in all his ways.

A double-minded man is a man who has not made up his mind. He vacillates back and forth between several opinions, and is not stable in any way.

Decide what you need and specify it.

Number two: *Lay Hold On It By Faith.*

Mark 11:23,24

For verily I say unto you, That whosoever shall say unto this mountain, Be thou removed, and be thou cast into the sea; and shall not doubt in his heart, but shall believe that those things which he saith shall come to pass; he shall have whatsoever he saith.

Therefore I say unto you, What things soever ye desire, when ye pray, believe that ye receive them, and ye shall have them.

That is how you exercise your faith. Decide what you need, be specific about it, then lay hold of it by faith saying, "I believe I have received."

Husbands and wives can do this by agreeing together according to Matthew 18:19.

Matthew 18:19

Again I say unto you, That if *two* of you shall agree on earth as touching any thing that *they* shall ask, it shall be done for *them* of my Father which is in heaven.

Husband and wife, here is an area where you can agree. You might not agree on the cat or the dog. You might not agree on the kind of food you are going to eat. But you can agree on the things of God. My wife and I did this, and we paid off our present home (a thirty-year mortgage) in three years. Praise God!

Number three: *Bind Satan's Power Over What Is Yours.*

We have already seen Malachi 3:11 where God will rebuke the devourer for our sakes. Mark 16:17 says, "Cast out the devil." James 4:7 tells us, "Resist the devil and he will flee from you."

In prayer you say: "Satan, in Jesus' name, I bind your power over what is mine. Take your hands off!" Then by faith see him obeying your command.

Number Four: *Loose The Forces Of Heaven.*

Hebrews 1:14 and Psalm 103:20 tells you about the angels. You have angels that are ministering spirits, sent forth to minister *for you*, just like waiters who are waiting the table. You tell them in prayer, in the Name of Jesus, to go out and act on your behalf.

Number Five: *Praise God For The Answer.*

Never forget to praise Him, in prayer, for the answer. Declare, say, and speak it, as though it were already done. Declare it as though it were already an accomplished fact, because as far as the spirit world is concerned, it is an accomplished fact.

10
Commonly Asked Questions On Tithes and Offerings

There are questions that have arisen because people have not been properly instructed. Let us consider some of them.

1. Can I Specify Where the Tithe Goes?

Some people say, "I am going to put my tithe in and specify where it goes, such as the TV Ministry, the Radio Ministry, etc."

You cannot specify where the tithe goes. You *can*, however, specify where the offering goes. Why? Because the offering belongs to you. It is your money. But the tithe belongs to the Lord; therefore, you have no right to say where it should go. It is up to the storehouse to determine where the tithe goes.

You cannot put your tithe in and say, "I want this tithe to go to the Television Ministry, or to the Building Fund, or to the Radio Ministry." You cannot tell the storehouse what to do with God's money. That 10% is not yours; it is God's. However, the remaining 90% is yours, and you can specify where it should go.

I put my tithe in; then *I* decide to support a TV Ministry that I believe in, so I put an offering in and specify TV. I can do that, because it is a part of that

90% which belongs to me; and I can do whatever I please with it. But I cannot do that with the tithe, because the tithe belongs to the Lord.

Remember Malachi 3:8,10: ''Will a man rob God? How have we robbed him? In tithes and offerings. Bring ye all the tithes into the storehouse.''

Notice, it mentions tithes and offerings, but the emphasis is on the tithes. ''Bring ye all the tithes, not all the tithes *and* offerings. In both of them you rob me.''

He said, ''Bring *all* the tithes into the storehouse and prove Me, and I will open the windows of heaven.'' He did not say, ''Bring the *offerings* in and I will open the windows of heaven.

The windows-of-heaven blessings come as a result of tithes, but you ought to give offerings too—and if you love Him, you will.

2. Can I Buy Things (Books, Tapes, etc.) with the Tithe?

One person told me that he would take the tithe, go to the bookstore, and buy tapes and books because it was good spiritual food.

You cannot do that. That would not be a tithe, but a purchase.

You cannot buy things with the tithe. It is not your money to spend—it belongs to the Lord! To buy books and tapes is good. You will be blessed by them, but that is not what the tithes are for. It would be inconsistent.

Remember, God said to bring all the tithes into *the storehouse*, not into the bookstore. Pay the tithe and use your 90% to buy tapes and books.

3. Should I Tithe Out of the Gross or the Net?

The gross is the total amount. The net is the amount left after all necessary deductions have been taken out.

How do we answer this question? The Bible does not tell us. You will not find a chapter in the Bible on gross and net (unless it is a fishing net!).

How do we figure it out? By simply using some wisdom. Let me give you an example.

I am classified as self-employed by the Internal Revenue Service, so I have to take out my own income taxes. Nobody sits down and deducts F.I.C.A. and other taxes from my check. Whatever I receive is always a gross amount; no deductions have been taken out. So I have no choice but to pay my tithes out of the gross, right off the top.

But what do *you* do if you work on a job where they take out deductions? Here is what I advise:

Keep in mind that the only money you actually have to spend is the money you get in your little hot hands. The rest are numbers on a check stub. You never get the actual unemployment insurance money, or the social security money, or the income tax money. They do not even ask you about that—they just take it out, and you end up with what is left over, right?

You have a piece of paper that says you made $300, but by the time they finish cutting it down, you have $145 left. That is all you actually receive. (We call it "net." But really it is *your* gross because that $145 is all you have to spend.) You did not receive the whole $300, but only $145. So I would say you should tithe out of the $145.

Here is what I did: When I was without a job, I made application and claimed unemployment insurance. They had taken that unemployment insurance out of my check weekly. I never did get that money in my hand, so I never actually had it to spend as mine. But when I started drawing my unemployment insurance money, then I tithed out of that.

It was the same with the income taxes. They took money out every week. I never received that money. It was never in my hand. I could not spend it, so I did not tithe out of it. However, when I received income tax money as a refund, I tithed out of that, because that money was actually mine.

If I were drawing social security, then I would tithe out of the social security. But I would not tithe out of it until I actually received it, because I cannot spend it until I get it. That is my suggestion to you.

Here is another situation: You may work on a job where you have a credit union. You decide to save some money, so you let the credit union take out $10 a week before you get the money in your hand. However, that is the same as your receiving it. That is *your* money, so you have to tithe out of it. You chose to have them collect it and hold it for you, so you have to treat it as though it were placed in your hand.

For instance, let us say you make $100. Your tithe is $10. The government takes out $10 for taxes and you decide to save $10 in your credit union. Actually all you receive in your hand is $80, but you have to treat it as though it were $90 and tithe out of the $90. That $90 is *your* money, and *you* had a choice as to how you wanted to spend it. It is your money, so you have to tithe out of it.

Suppose you buy an automobile through the credit union. The credit union is taking the payments out. You have to treat that as though you received it in your hands. You had a choice. The credit union did not *have* to take the money out of your check, but *you* chose to do it that way. Let them take it out, but you still have to treat it as though you received the money personally.

You have no choice about the money the government takes. But the money deducted by the credit union is a decision you make. You have to treat it as part of the money you actually receive in your hands. Can you see that?

Someone says, "I do not agree with Brother Price. I think I ought to tithe out of the gross." Wonderful! You cannot give God too much, so I would not argue about it. But I know of a situation where a young man was tithing out of the gross and it was strapping him. His family was struggling. He wanted to be obedient to the Lord and he thought he had to tithe out of the gross. That is okay when you reach a point where you can afford to tithe on the gross.

I am simply saying you do not *have* to tithe the gross. Tithe the net—that is *all* you actually receive.

And that is all you can actually spend.

If you want to tithe the gross, go ahead. You cannot give God too much. Do not get into a situation where you are in bondage over this. God does not want you to be in bondage, He wants you to be free. So be free and enjoy the freedom!

Dr. Frederick K.C. Price is the founder and pastor of Crenshaw Christian Center in Los Angeles, California, which has a rapidly growing membership of over 13,000.

Dr. Price is in great demand as a seminar teacher. He travels throughout the world  teaching the Word simply and in the power of the Holy Spirit. His ministry includes radio programs throughout the country and a weekly one-hour television broadcast, "Ever Increasing Faith," which airs throughout the United States, Haiti, Australia, the Bahamas, South Africa, and the Virgin Islands.

Dr. Price's God-given ability as a teacher enables him to simply and understandably transmit to others how faith works.

For a complete list of tapes and books by Fred Price, or to receive his publication, *Ever Increasing Faith Messenger*, write:

Fred Price
Crenshaw Christian Center
P. O. Box 90000
Los Angeles, CA 90009

*Feel free to include your prayer requests
and comments when you write.*